To:

_____

From:

_____

Date:

_____

Published by Christian Art Publishers
PO Box 1599, Vereeniging, 1930, RSA

© 2021
First edition 2021

Designed by Christian Art Publishers

Images used under license from Shutterstock.com

Scripture quotations are taken from the *Holy Bible*,
King James Version, and is in the public domain.

Printed in China

ISBN 978-1-4321-3492-1

21 22 23 24 25 26 27 28 29 30 – 10 9 8 7 6 5 4 3 2 1

Promises to STRENGTHEN YOUR FAITH

KING JAMES VERSION

CHRISTIAN ART
PUBLISHERS

Contents

Acceptance

Ye were sealed with that holy Spirit
of promise, which is the earnest of
our inheritance until the redemption
of the purchased possession,
unto the praise of his glory.
EPHESIANS 1:13-14

Wherefore receive ye one another,
as Christ also received us
to the glory of God.
ROMANS 15:7

The words of a wise man's
mouth are gracious.
ECCLESIASTES 10:12

God created man in his own image.
GENESIS 1:27

A good name is rather to be chosen than great riches, and loving favour rather than silver and gold.
PROVERBS 22:1

*F*or thou, LORD, wilt bless the righteous; with favour wilt thou compass him as with a shield.
PSALM 5:12

*A*ll that the Father giveth me shall come to me; and him that cometh to me I will in no wise cast out.
JOHN 6:37

*I*f thou doest well, shalt thou not be accepted?
GENESIS 4:7

For do I now persuade men,
or God? or do I seek to please men?
for if I yet pleased men, I should
not be the servant of Christ.
GALATIANS 1:10

Study to shew thyself approved
unto God, a workman that needeth
not to be ashamed, rightly
dividing the word of truth.
2 TIMOTHY 2:15

The LORD is good to all: and his
tender mercies are over all his works.
PSALM 145:9

Let not mercy and truth forsake thee:
bind them about thy neck;
write them upon the table of
thine heart: So shalt thou find
favour and good understanding
in the sight of God and man.
PROVERBS 3:3-4

Affection

Yea, I have loved thee with an
everlasting love: therefore with
lovingkindness have I drawn thee.
JEREMIAH 31:3

Casting all your care upon
him; for he careth for you.
1 PETER 5:7

The LORD thy God in the midst
of thee is mighty; he will save,
he will rejoice over thee with joy;
he will rest in his love, he will
joy over thee with singing.
ZEPHANIAH 3:17

Know therefore that
the Lord thy God, he is God,
the faithful God,
which keepeth covenant
and mercy with them that love
him and keep his commandments
to a thousand generations.
DEUTERONOMY 7:9

He shall feed his flock like
a shepherd: he shall gather
the lambs with his arm,
and carry them in his bosom.
ISAIAH 40:11

Are not two sparrows sold for
a farthing? and one of them shall
not fall on the ground without your
Father. Fear ye not therefore, ye are
of more value than many sparrows.
MATTHEW 10:29, 31

But thou, O Lord, art a God
full of compassion, and gracious,
long suffering, and plenteous
in mercy and truth.
PSALM 86:15

For, behold, I am for you,
and I will turn unto you.
EZEKIEL 36:9

I am like a green olive tree in
the house of God: I trust in the
mercy of God for ever and ever.
PSALM 52:8

God, who is rich in mercy, for his
great love wherewith he loved us,
even when we were dead in sins, hath
quickened us together with Christ.
EPHESIANS 2:4-5

Be kindly affectioned one to
another with brotherly love; in
honour preferring one another.
ROMANS 12:10

Behold, what manner of love the
Father hath bestowed upon us, that
we should be called the sons of God.
1 JOHN 3:1

Assurance

Your Father knoweth that
ye have need of these things.
LUKE 12:30

Behold, I give unto you power
to tread on serpents and scorpions,
and over all the power of the enemy:
and nothing shall by any means hurt you.
LUKE 10:19

Our help is in the name of the LORD,
who made heaven and earth.
PSALM 124:8

I am come that they might have life,
and that they might have
it more abundantly.
JOHN 10:10

Nay, in all these things
we are more than conquerors
through him that loved us.
ROMANS 8:37

*L*et us draw near with a true heart
in full assurance of faith,
having our hearts sprinkled from
an evil conscience, and our bodies
washed with pure water.
HEBREWS 10:22

*H*e is the LORD our God: his judgments
are in all the earth. He hath remembered
his covenant for ever, the word which he
commanded to a thousand generations.
PSALM 105:7-8

*T*he LORD is my light and my salvation;
whom shall I fear? the LORD is the strength
of my life; of whom shall I be afraid?
PSALM 27:1

*V*erily, verily, I say unto you, he that
heareth my word, and believeth on
him that sent me, hath everlasting life,
and shall not come into condemnation;
but is passed from death unto life.
JOHN 5:24

*A*s far as the east is from
the west, so far hath he removed
our transgressions from us.
PSALM 103:12

For thou hast maintained my
right and my cause; thou satest
in the throne judging right.
PSALM 9:4

For the eyes of the LORD run to
and fro throughout the whole earth,
to shew himself strong in the behalf of
them whose heart is perfect toward him.
2 CHRONICLES 16:9

He that hath my commandments,
and keepeth them, he it is that loveth me:
and he that loveth me shall be loved
of my Father, and I will love him,
and will manifest myself to him.
JOHN 14:21

And therefore will the LORD wait,
that he may be gracious unto you,
and therefore will he be exalted, that
he may have mercy upon you: for the
Lord is a God of judgment: blessed
are all they that wait for him.
ISAIAH 30:18

The Lord knoweth how to deliver
the godly out of temptations.
2 PETER 2:9

There hath no temptation taken you
but such as is common to man:
but God is faithful, who will not suffer
you to be tempted above that ye are
able; but will with the temptation
also make a way to escape, that
ye may be able to bear it.
1 CORINTHIANS 10:13

For I am persuaded, that neither death,
nor life, nor angels, nor principalities,
nor powers, nor things present, nor
things to come, nor height, nor depth,
nor any other creature, shall be able
to separate us from the love of God,
which is in Christ Jesus our Lord.
ROMANS 8:38-39

But the God of all grace, who hath
called us unto his eternal glory by
Christ Jesus, after that ye have suffered
a while, make you perfect, stablish,
strengthen, settle you. To him be glory
and dominion for ever and ever. Amen.
1 PETER 5:10-11

He that loveth his brother abideth
in the light, and there is none
occasion of stumbling in him.
1 JOHN 2:10

Balance

$\mathcal{B}$e perfect, be of good comfort, be of
one mind, live in peace; and the God
of love and peace shall be with you.
2 CORINTHIANS 13:11

$\mathcal{W}$hatsoever thy hand findeth
to do, do it with thy might.
ECCLESIASTES 9:10

$\mathcal{T}$o every thing there is a season,
and a time to every purpose
under the heaven.
ECCLESIASTES 3:1

$\mathcal{G}$ive me neither poverty nor riches;
feed me with food convenient for me.
PROVERBS 30:8

$\mathcal{F}$or what is a man profited,
if he shall gain the whole world,
and lose his own soul?
MATTHEW 16:26

I can do all things through
Christ which strengtheneth me.
PHILIPPIANS 4:13

Our soul waiteth for the LORD:
he is our help and our shield.
PSALM 33:20

I have learned, in whatsoever state
I am, therewith to be content.
PHILIPPIANS 4:11

I trusted in thee, O LORD: I said, thou
art my God. My times are in thy hand.
PSALM 31:14-15

Let the beauty of the LORD our God
be upon us: and establish thou the
work of our hands upon us; yea, the
work of our hands establish thou it.
PSALM 90:17

If we live in the Spirit, let us
also walk in the Spirit.
GALATIANS 5:25

Freely ye have received,
freely give.
MATTHEW 10:8

Blessings

The LORD is the portion of mine
inheritance and of my cup.
PSALM 16:5

It is of the LORD's mercies that
we are not consumed, because his
compassions fail not. They are new every
morning: great is thy faithfulness.
LAMENTATIONS 3:22-23

For the LORD God is a sun and
shield: the LORD will give grace and
glory: no good thing will he withhold
from them that walk uprightly.
PSALM 84:11

Thou openest thine hand, and satisfiest
the desire of every living thing.
PSALM 145:16

Blessed are the pure in heart:
for they shall see God.
MATTHEW 5:8

Remember the words of the
Lord Jesus, how he said, It is more
blessed to give than to receive.
ACTS 20:35

The LORD thy God shall bless thee
in all thine increase, and in all the
works of thine hands, therefore
thou shalt surely rejoice.
DEUTERONOMY 16:15

My cup runneth over. Surely
goodness and mercy shall follow
me all the days of my life.
PSALM 23:5-6

O taste and see that the LORD is good:
blessed is the man that trusteth in him.
PSALM 34:8

Thou hast beset me behind and before,
and laid thine hand upon me.
PSALM 139:5

The same LORD over all is rich
unto all that call upon him.
ROMANS 10:12

The LORD will bless
his people with peace.
PSALM 29:11

Blessed be the God and Father
of our Lord Jesus Christ, who hath
blessed us with all spiritual blessings
in heavenly places in Christ.
EPHESIANS 1:3

The LORD is the portion of mine
inheritance and of my cup: thou
maintainest my lot. The lines are
fallen unto me in pleasant places;
yea, I have a goodly heritage.
PSALM 16:5-6

They that seek the LORD shall
not want any good thing.
PSALM 34:10

Blessed are the poor in spirit:
for theirs is the kingdom of heaven.
Blessed are they that mourn:
for they shall be comforted. Blessed are
the meek: for they shall inherit the earth.
Blessed are they which do hunger and
thirst after righteousness: for they shall
be filled. Blessed are the merciful:
for they shall obtain mercy. Blessed are
the pure in heart: for they shall see God.
Blessed are the peacemakers:
for they shall be called the
children of God. Blessed are they which
are persecuted for righteousness' sake:
for theirs is the kingdom of heaven.
Blessed are ye, when men shall revile
you, and persecute you, and shall say
all manner of evil against you falsely,
for my sake. Rejoice, and be exceeding
glad: for great is your reward in heaven.
MATTHEW 5:3-12

Career

Be ye stedfast, unmoveable,
always abounding in the work
of the Lord, forasmuch as
ye know that your labour is
not in vain in the Lord.
1 CORINTHIANS 15:58

Give diligence to make your calling
and election sure: for if ye do these
things, ye shall never fall.
2 PETER 1:10

Grant thee according to thine own
heart, and fulfil all thy counsel.
PSALM 20:4

The LORD shall open unto thee his
good treasure, the heaven to give the
rain unto thy land in his season, and
to bless all the work of thine hand.
DEUTERONOMY 28:12

Challenges

Count it all joy when ye fall into divers temptations; knowing this, that the trying of your faith worketh patience. But let patience have her perfect work, that ye may be perfect and entire, wanting nothing.
JAMES 1:2-4

In the world ye shall have tribulation: but be of good cheer; I have overcome the world.
JOHN 16:33

For I the LORD thy God will hold thy right hand, saying unto thee, Fear not; I will help thee.
ISAIAH 41:13

While we look not at the things which are seen, but at the things which are not seen: for the things which are seen are temporal; but the things which are not seen are eternal.
2 CORINTHIANS 4:18

Is any among you afflicted? let him pray.
JAMES 5:13

Blessed is the man that endureth temptation: for when he is tried, he shall receive the crown of life, which the Lord hath promised to them that love him.
JAMES 1:12

I can do all things through Christ which strengtheneth me.
PHILIPPIANS 4:13

*L*et us lay aside every weight, and
the sin which doth so easily beset
us, and let us run with patience
the race that is set before us.
HEBREWS 12:1

*W*herein ye greatly rejoice, though
now for a season, if need be, ye are in
heaviness through manifold temptations.
1 PETER 1:6

*E*xamine me, O LORD, and prove
me; try my reins and my heart.
PSALM 26:2

*B*e strong and of good courage,
and do it: fear not, nor be dismayed:
for the LORD God, even my God,
will be with thee; he will not
fail thee, nor forsake thee.
1 CHRONICLES 28:20

*A*sk, and it shall be given you;
seek, and ye shall find; knock,
and it shall be opened unto you.
LUKE 11:9

Character

Whatsoever things are true, whatsoever
things are honest, whatsoever things
are just, whatsoever things are pure,
whatsoever things are lovely, whatsoever
things are of good report; if there be any
virtue, and if there be any praise, think
on these things. Those things, which
ye have both learned, and received,
and heard, and seen in me, do: and
the God of peace shall be with you.
PHILIPPIANS 4:8-9

Be ye therefore followers of God,
as dear children; and walk in love,
as Christ also hath loved us.
EPHESIANS 5:1-2

Whoso keepeth his mouth
and his tongue keepeth
his soul from troubles.
PROVERBS 21:23

Let your speech be always with
grace, seasoned with salt.
COLOSSIANS 4:6

The tree is known by his fruit.
MATTHEW 12:33

For God giveth to a man
that is good in his sight wisdom,
and knowledge, and joy.
ECCLESIASTES 2:26

Create in me a clean heart, O God;
and renew a right spirit within me.
PSALM 51:10

For every tree is known by
his own fruit. A good man out of
the good treasure of his heart
bringeth forth that which is good.
LUKE 6:44-45

$\mathcal{F}$ollow after righteousness,
godliness, faith, love, patience,
meekness. Fight the good fight of faith.
1 TIMOTHY 6:11-12

$\mathcal{T}$hou through thy commandments hast
made me wiser than mine enemies.
PSALM 119:98

$\mathcal{H}$umble yourselves in the sight of
the Lord, and he shall lift you up.
JAMES 4:10

$\mathcal{B}$e strong in the grace
that is in Christ Jesus.
2 TIMOTHY 2:1

$\mathcal{B}$efore I formed thee in the belly
I knew thee; and before thou camest
forth out of the womb I sanctified thee.
JEREMIAH 1:5

$\mathcal{G}$lory, honour, and peace,
to every man that worketh good.
ROMANS 2:10

*W*herewithal shall a young man cleanse his way? by taking heed thereto according to thy word.
PSALM 119:9

*F*or it is God which worketh in you both to will and to do of his good pleasure.
PHILIPPIANS 2:13

*L*et patience have her perfect work, that ye may be perfect and entire, wanting nothing.
JAMES 1:4

*P*ut on therefore, as the elect of God, holy and beloved, bowels of mercies, kindness, humbleness of mind, meekness, longsuffering.
COLOSSIANS 3:12

*B*lessed be God, even the Father of our Lord Jesus Christ, the Father of mercies, and the God of all comfort; who comforteth us in all our tribulation, that we may be able to comfort them which are in any trouble, by the comfort wherewith we ourselves are comforted of God.
2 CORINTHIANS 1:3-4

Church

The church of the living God, the
pillar and ground of the truth.
1 TIMOTHY 3:15

Let us therefore follow after the things
which make for peace, and things
wherewith one may edify another.
ROMANS 14:19

Knowledge puffeth up,
but charity edifieth.
1 CORINTHIANS 8:1

But speaking the truth in love, [we]
may grow up into him in all things, which
is the head, even Christ: From whom
the whole body fitly joined together.
EPHESIANS 4:15

So we, being many, are one
body in Christ, and every one
members one of another.
ROMANS 12:5

That ye all speak the same thing,
and that there be no divisions among you;
but that ye be perfectly joined together in
the same mind and in the same judgment.
1 CORINTHIANS 1:10

For other foundation can no man lay
than that is laid, which is Jesus Christ.
1 CORINTHIANS 3:11

All that believed were together,
and had all things common; and sold
their possessions and goods, and parted
them to all men, as every man had need.
And they, continuing daily with one
accord in the temple, and breaking bread
from house to house, did eat their meat
with gladness and singleness of heart,
praising God, and having favour with all
the people. And the Lord added to the
church daily such as should be saved.
ACTS 2:44-47

Comfort

As one whom his mother
comforteth, so will I comfort you;
and ye shall be comforted.
ISAIAH 66:13

For the LORD will not cast off his people,
neither will he forsake his inheritance.
PSALM 94:14

Be still, and know that I am God: I
will be exalted among the heathen,
I will be exalted in the earth.
PSALM 46:10

Blessed be God, even the Father of
our Lord Jesus Christ, the Father of
mercies, and the God of all comfort;
who comforteth us in all our tribulation.
2 CORINTHIANS 1:3-4

Behold, I have graven thee
upon the palms of my hands.
ISAIAH 49:16

I, even I, am he that comforteth you:
who art thou, that thou shouldest
be afraid of a man that shall die,
and of the son of man which
shall be made as grass.
ISAIAH 51:12

*W*e know that all things work together for
good to them that love God, to them who
are the called according to his purpose.
ROMANS 8:28

*T*he LORD upholdeth all that fall,
and raiseth up all those
that be bowed down.
PSALM 145:14

*W*hen thou passest through the waters,
I will be with thee; and through the
rivers, they shall not overflow thee:
when thou walkest through the fire,
thou shalt not be burned; neither shall
the flame kindle upon thee. For I am
the LORD thy God, the Holy One.
ISAIAH 43:2-3

Compassion

The LORD is good to all: and his tender
mercies are over all his works.
PSALM 145:9

Therefore will the LORD wait, that he may
be gracious unto you, and therefore will he
be exalted, that he may have mercy upon
you: for the LORD is a God of judgment:
blessed are all they that wait for him.
ISAIAH 30:18

Blessed be God, even the Father of
our Lord Jesus Christ, the Father of
mercies, and the God of all comfort;
who comforteth us in all our
tribulation, that we may be able
to comfort them which are in any
trouble, by the comfort wherewith
we ourselves are comforted of God.
2 CORINTHIANS 1:3-4

The Lord make you to increase
and abound in love one toward
another, and toward all men,
even as we do toward you.
1 Thessalonians 3:12

The Lord is very pitiful,
and of tender mercy.
James 5:11

The Lord is merciful
and gracious, slow to anger,
and plenteous in mercy.
Psalm 103:8

As the Father hath loved me,
so have I loved you:
continue ye in my love.
John 15:9

Be ye therefore merciful,
as your Father also is merciful.
Luke 6:36

*G*reat are thy tender mercies,
O Lord: quicken me
according to thy judgments.
Psalm 119:156

*F*or the Lord hath comforted
his people, and will have
mercy upon his afflicted.
Isaiah 49:13

*T*he Lord your God is
gracious and merciful.
2 Chronicles 30:9

*U*nto the upright there ariseth
light in the darkness:
he is gracious, and full of
compassion, and righteous.
Psalm 112:4

Confidence

It is better to trust in the LORD
than to put confidence in man.
PSALM 118:8

This is the confidence that we have
in him, that, if we ask any thing
according to his will, he heareth us.
1 JOHN 5:14

Have not I commanded thee?
Be strong and of a good courage;
be not afraid, neither be thou
dismayed: for the LORD thy God is
with thee whithersoever thou goest.
JOSHUA 1:9

The LORD is my shepherd; I shall not want. He maketh me to lie down in green pastures: he leadeth me beside the still waters. He restoreth my soul: he leadeth me in the paths of righteousness for his name's sake.
PSALM 23:1-3

In the fear of the LORD is strong confidence: and his children shall have a place of refuge.
PROVERBS 14:26

If our heart condemn us not, then have we confidence toward God.
1 JOHN 3:21

For the LORD shall be thy confidence, and shall keep thy foot from being taken.
PROVERBS 3:26

I have set the Lord always before me: because he is at my right hand, I shall not be moved.
PSALM 16:8

*B*eing confident of this very thing, that he which hath begun a good work in you will perform it until the day of Jesus Christ.
PHILIPPIANS 1:6

*B*lessed is the man that trusteth in the Lord, and whose hope the Lord is.
JEREMIAH 17:7

*F*or we are made partakers of Christ, if we hold the beginning of our confidence stedfast unto the end.
HEBREWS 3:14

Contentment

$\mathscr{B}$etter is the sight of the eyes than
the wandering of the desire.
ECCLESIASTES 6:9

$\mathscr{L}$et your conversation be without
covetousness; and be content
with such things as ye have.
HEBREWS 13:5

$\mathscr{T}$he fear of the LORD tendeth to life:
and he that hath it shall abide satisfied;
he shall not be visited with evil.
PROVERBS 19:23

$\mathscr{W}$herefore laying aside all malice,
and all guile, and hypocrisies, and
envies, and all evil speakings.
1 PETER 2:1

Be careful for nothing; but in every thing by prayer and supplication with thanksgiving let your requests be made known unto God. And the peace of God, which passeth all understanding, shall keep your hearts and minds through Christ Jesus.
PHILIPPIANS 4:6-7

Take no thought for your life, what ye shall eat, or what ye shall drink; nor yet for your body, what ye shall put on. Is not the life more than meat, and the body than raiment?
MATTHEW 6:25

We should live soberly, righteously, and godly, in this present world.
TITUS 2:12

LORD, thou wilt ordain
peace for us: for thou also hast
wrought all our works in us.
ISAIAH 26:12

Thou shalt not covet thy neighbour's
house, thou shalt not covet thy neighbour's
wife, nor his manservant, nor his
maidservant, nor his ox, nor his ass,
nor any thing that is thy neighbour's.
EXODUS 20:17

A sound heart is the life of the flesh.
PROVERBS 14:30

Godliness with
contentment is great gain.
1 TIMOTHY 6:6

I have learned, in whatsoever state
I am, therewith to be content.
I know both how to be abased,
and I know how to abound:
every where and in all things
I am instructed both to be full
and to be hungry, both to
abound and to suffer need.
PHILIPPIANS 4:11-12

Courage

Be of good courage, and he
shall strengthen your heart, all
ye that hope in the LORD.
PSALM 31:24

Be strong in the grace that
is in Christ Jesus.
2 TIMOTHY 2:1

But straightway Jesus spake
unto them, saying, Be of good
cheer; it is I; be not afraid.
MATTHEW 14:27

The LORD thy God is among you,
a mighty God and terrible.
DEUTERONOMY 7:21

By my God have I leaped over a wall.
PSALM 18:29

Watch ye, stand fast in the faith,
quit you like men, be strong.
1 CORINTHIANS 16:13

Be strong and of a good courage;
be not afraid, neither be thou
dismayed: for the LORD thy God is
with thee whithersoever thou goest.
JOSHUA 1:9

The LORD is my light and my salvation;
whom shall I fear? the LORD is the strength
of my life; of whom shall I be afraid?
PSALM 27:1

For he shall give his angels
charge over thee, to keep thee
in all thy ways. They shall bear
thee up in their hands, lest thou
dash thy foot against a stone.
PSALM 91:11-12

In the day when I cried thou
answeredst me, and strengthenedst
me with strength in my soul.
PSALM 138:3

For God hath not given us the
spirit of fear; but of power, and
of love, and of a sound mind.
2 TIMOTHY 1:7

Decisions

Rejoice, O young man, in thy youth;
and let thy heart cheer thee in the days
of thy youth, and walk in the ways of
thine heart, and in the sight of thine eyes:
but know thou, that for all these things
God will bring thee into judgment.
ECCLESIASTES 11:9

For this God is our God
for ever and ever: he will be
our guide even unto death.
PSALM 48:14

When wisdom entereth into thine heart,
and knowledge is pleasant unto thy
soul; discretion shall preserve thee,
understanding shall keep thee:
to deliver thee from the way of
the evil man, from the man that
speaketh froward things.
PROVERBS 2:10-12

Commit thy works unto the LORD, and
thy thoughts shall be established.
PROVERBS 16:3

Walk in the Spirit, and ye shall
not fulfil the lust of the flesh.
GALATIANS 5:16

But it is good for me
to draw near to God:
I have put my trust in the Lord God,
that I may declare all thy works.
PSALM 73:28

For thou wilt light my candle: the LORD
my God will enlighten my darkness.
PSALM 18:28

In thee, O Lord, do I put my trust:
let me never be put to confusion.
PSALM 71:1

If any of you lack wisdom, let him ask of
God, that giveth to all men liberally, and
upbraideth not; and it shall be given him.
JAMES 1:5

Discretion shall preserve thee,
understanding shall keep thee.
PROVERBS 2:11

There are many devices in a man's
heart; nevertheless the counsel
of the Lord, that shall stand.
PROVERBS 19:21

The lot is cast into the lap; but the whole
disposing thereof is of the Lord.
PROVERBS 16:33

Dependability

Happy is he that hath the God of Jacob for his help, whose hope is in the LORD his God: which made heaven, and earth, the sea, and all that therein is: which keepeth truth for ever.
PSALM 146:5-6

Cast thy burden upon the LORD, and he shall sustain thee: he shall never suffer the righteous to be moved.
PSALM 55:22

Whosoever believeth on him shall not be ashamed.
ROMANS 10:11

That by two immutable things, in which it was impossible for God to lie, we might have a strong consolation, who have fled for refuge to lay hold upon the hope set before us.
HEBREWS 6:18

Then spake Jesus again unto them,
saying, I am the light of the world: he
that followeth me shall not walk in
darkness, but shall have the light of life.
JOHN 8:12

Let not mercy and truth forsake thee:
bind them about thy neck; write them
upon the table of thine heart: so shalt
thou find favour and good understanding
in the sight of God and man.
PROVERBS 3:3-4

It is better to trust in the LORD
than to put confidence in princes.
PSALM 118:9

So that we may boldly say, the
Lord is my helper, and I will not
fear what man shall do unto me.
HEBREWS 13:6

Render therefore to all their dues:
tribute to whom tribute is due;
custom to whom custom; fear to whom
fear; honour to whom honour.
ROMANS 13:7

Be ye mindful always of his covenant;
the word which he commanded
to a thousand generations.
1 CHRONICLES 16:15

God is not a man, that he should
lie; neither the son of man, that he
should repent: hath he said, and
shall he not do it? or hath he spoken,
and shall he not make it good?
NUMBERS 23:19

And now, Lord, what wait
I for? my hope is in thee.
PSALM 39:7

Discipleship

Ye are the light of the world.
A city that is set on an hill cannot be hid.
Neither do men light a candle,
and put it under a bushel, but on a
candlestick; and it giveth light unto
all that are in the house. Let your
light so shine before men, that they
may see your good works, and glorify
your Father which is in heaven.
MATTHEW 5:14-16

And he said to them all,
If any man will come after me,
let him deny himself, and take up
his cross daily, and follow me.
LUKE 9:23

Let him that is taught in the
word communicate unto him that
teacheth in all good things.
GALATIANS 6:6

Go ye therefore, and teach
all nations, baptizing them in the
name of the Father, and of the
Son, and of the Holy Ghost.
MATTHEW 28:19

Whosoever he be of you that
forsaketh not all that he hath,
he cannot be my disciple.
LUKE 14:33

As he spake these words, many believed
on him. Then said Jesus to those Jews
which believed on him, If ye continue
in my word, then are ye my disciples
indeed; and ye shall know the truth,
and the truth shall make you free.
JOHN 8:30-32

Be ye followers of me,
even as I also am of Christ.
1 CORINTHIANS 11:1

He said unto them, Go ye into
all the world, and preach the
gospel to every creature.
MARK 16:15

Encouragement

Blessed be the God and Father of our Lord Jesus Christ, which according to his abundant mercy hath begotten us again unto a lively hope by the resurrection of Jesus Christ from the dead, to an inheritance incorruptible, and undefiled, and that fadeth not away, reserved in heaven for you.
1 Peter 1:3-4

Be not conformed to this world: but be ye transformed by the renewing of your mind, that ye may prove what is that good, and acceptable, and perfect, will of God.
Romans 12:2

Wherefore gird up the loins of your mind, be sober, and hope to the end for the grace that is to be brought unto you at the revelation of Jesus Christ.
1 Peter 1:13

For whatsoever things were written aforetime were written for our learning, that we through patience and comfort of the scriptures might have hope.
ROMANS 15:4

He that dwelleth in the secret place of the most High shall abide under the shadow of the Almighty. I will say of the LORD, He is my refuge and my fortress: my God; in him will I trust.
PSALM 91:1-2

Be ye strong therefore, and let not your hands be weak: for your work shall be rewarded.
1 CHRONICLES 15:7

In the world ye shall have tribulation: but be of good cheer; I have overcome the world.
JOHN 16:33

In whom also we have obtained an inheritance, being predestinated according to the purpose of him who worketh all things after the counsel of his own will.
EPHESIANS 1:11

If thou canst believe, all things are possible to him that believeth.
MARK 9:23

The LORD shall preserve thy going out and thy coming in from this time forth, and even for evermore.
PSALM 121:8

As for God, his way is perfect: the word of the LORD is tried: he is a buckler to all those that trust in him.
PSALM 18:30

The LORD, he it is that doth go before thee; he will be with thee, he will not fail thee, neither forsake thee.
DEUTERONOMY 31:8

Eternal Life

He that believeth on the Son
hath everlasting life.
JOHN 3:36

For God so loved the world, that
he gave his only begotten Son, that
whosoever believeth in him should not
perish, but have everlasting life.
JOHN 3:16

And this is the will of him that
sent me, that every one which
seeth the Son, and believeth on
him, may have everlasting life.
JOHN 6:40

My sheep hear my voice, and I know
them, and they follow me: And I
give unto them eternal life; and they
shall never perish, neither shall any
man pluck them out of my hand.
JOHN 10:27-28

The gift of God is eternal life
through Jesus Christ our Lord.
ROMANS 6:23

Let not your heart be troubled: ye
believe in God, believe also in me. In
my Father's house are many mansions:
if it were not so, I would have told you.
I go to prepare a place for you. And if
I go and prepare a place for you, I will
come again, and receive you unto myself;
that where I am, there ye may be also.
JOHN 14:1-3

Lay not up for yourselves treasures
upon earth, where moth and rust doth
corrupt, and where thieves break
through and steal: but lay up for
yourselves treasures in heaven, where
neither moth nor rust doth corrupt, and
where thieves do not break through
nor steal: for where your treasure
is, there will your heart be also.
MATTHEW 6:19-21

In this was manifested the love of
God toward us, because that God sent
his only begotten Son into the world,
that we might live through him.
1 JOHN 4:9

They that have done good,
unto the resurrection of life.
JOHN 5:29

Keep yourselves in the love of God,
looking for the mercy of our Lord
Jesus Christ unto eternal life.
JUDE 21

Verily, verily, I say unto you,
he that believeth on me
hath everlasting life.
JOHN 6:47

Excellence

Thus will I magnify myself,
and sanctify myself; and I will be
known in the eyes of many nations,
and they shall know that I am the Lord.
Ezekiel 38:23

Let your light so shine before men,
that they may see your good works,
and glorify your Father
which is in heaven.
Matthew 5:16

Even so ye, forasmuch as ye are zealous
of spiritual gifts, seek that ye may
excel to the edifying of the church.
1 Corinthians 14:12

Praise him for his mighty acts:
praise him according to his
excellent greatness.
Psalm 150:2

For I know that the LORD is great,
and that our LORD is above all gods.
PSALM 135:5

He hath shewed thee, O man, what is
good; and what doth the LORD require of
thee, but to do justly, and to love mercy,
and to walk humbly with thy God?
MICAH 6:8

Whatsoever things are true,
whatsoever things are honest,
whatsoever things are just,
whatsoever things are pure,
whatsoever things are lovely,
whatsoever things are of good report;
if there be any virtue, and if there be
any praise, think on these things.
PHILIPPIANS 4:8

Yea, the LORD shall give
that which is good.
PSALM 85:12

*Y*ea, if thou criest after knowledge,
and liftest up thy voice
for understanding; if thou seekest
her as silver, and searchest for her
as for hid treasures; then shalt thou
understand the fear of the LORD,
and find the knowledge of God.
PROVERBS 2:3-5

*A*ccording as his divine power
hath given unto us all things that
pertain unto life and godliness,
through the knowledge of him that
hath called us to glory and virtue.
2 PETER 1:3

I know also, my God, that thou triest the
heart, and hast pleasure in uprightness.
1 CHRONICLES 29:17

*B*ut the path of the just is as the
shining light, that shineth more
and more unto the perfect day.
PROVERBS 4:18

Fairness

The judgments of the LORD are
true and righteous altogether.
PSALM 19:9

He is the Rock, his work is perfect:
for all his ways are judgment:
a God of truth and without
iniquity, just and right is he.
DEUTERONOMY 32:4

Thus saith the LORD, Keep ye
judgment, and do justice.
ISAIAH 56:1

And if ye call on the Father,
who without respect of persons
judgeth according to every man's
work, pass the time of your
sojourning here in fear.
1 PETER 1:17

The LORD your God is God of gods,
and Lord of lords, a great God,
a mighty, and a terrible, which
regardeth not persons.
DEUTERONOMY 10:17

The works of his hands are verity
and judgment; all his
commandments are sure.
PSALM 111:7

Forbearing one another,
and forgiving one another,
if any man have a quarrel
against any: even as Christ
forgave you, so also do ye.
COLOSSIANS 3:13

He will regard the prayer of the
destitute, and not despise their prayer.
PSALM 102:17

Thou shalt not avenge, nor bear
any grudge against the children
of thy people, but thou shalt love
thy neighbour as thyself.
LEVITICUS 19:18

Now no chastening for the present
seemeth to be joyous, but grievous:
nevertheless afterward it yieldeth the
peaceable fruit of righteousness unto
them which are exercised thereby.
HEBREWS 12:11

But when we are judged, we are
chastened of the Lord, that we should
not be condemned with the world.
1 CORINTHIANS 11:32

Then shall ye call upon me,
and ye shall go and pray unto me,
and I will hearken unto you.
JEREMIAH 29:12

Faith

*N*ow faith is the substance of things
hoped for, the evidence of things not seen.
HEBREWS 11:1

*L*ooking unto Jesus the author
and finisher of our faith.
HEBREWS 12:2

*B*lessed are they that have not
seen, and yet have believed.
JOHN 20:29

*V*erily, verily, I say unto you, He that
heareth my word, and believeth on him
that sent me, hath everlasting life.
JOHN 5:24

*F*or verily I say unto you, If ye have
faith as a grain of mustard seed,
ye shall say unto this mountain,
Remove hence to yonder place;
and it shall remove; and nothing
shall be impossible unto you.
MATTHEW 17:20

Be still, and know that I am God: I
will be exalted among the heathen,
I will be exalted in the earth.
PSALM 46:10

He that believeth on me, believeth
not on me, but on him that sent me.
And he that seeth me seeth him that
sent me. I am come a light into the
world, that whosoever believeth on
me should not abide in darkness.
JOHN 12:44-46

For we are made partakers of Christ,
if we hold the beginning of our
confidence stedfast unto the end.
HEBREWS 3:14

As ye have therefore received
Christ Jesus the Lord, so walk ye in him:
rooted and built up in him,
and stablished in the faith, as
ye have been taught, abounding
therein with thanksgiving.
COLOSSIANS 2:6-7

And now abideth faith, hope,
charity, these three.
1 CORINTHIANS 13:13

That the eyes of your understanding
being enlightened; that ye may know
what is the hope of his calling, and
what the riches of the glory of his
inheritance in the saints, and what is
the exceeding greatness of his power
to us-ward who believe, according to
the working of his mighty power.
EPHESIANS 1:18-19

For verily I say unto you,
That whosoever shall say unto this
mountain, Be thou removed, and be thou
cast into the sea; and shall not doubt in
his heart, but shall believe that those
things which he saith shall come to pass;
he shall have whatsoever he saith.
MARK 11:23

But without faith it is impossible
to please him: for he that cometh to
God must believe that he is, and
that he is a rewarder of them
that diligently seek him.
HEBREWS 11:6

Family

For whosoever shall do the will
of God, the same is my brother,
and my sister, and mother.
MARK 3:35

Honour thy father and thy mother:
that thy days may be long upon the land
which the LORD thy God giveth thee.
EXODUS 20:12

And will be a Father unto you,
and ye shall be my sons and
daughters, saith the Lord Almighty.
2 CORINTHIANS 6:18

Wherefore thou art no more a
servant, but a son; and if a son, then
an heir of God through Christ.
GALATIANS 4:7

*L*ike as a father pitieth his children,
so the LORD pitieth them that fear him.
PSALM 103:13

*T*rain up a child in the way he
should go: and when he is old,
he will not depart from it.
PROVERBS 22:6

*M*y son, keep thy father's commandment,
and forsake not the law of thy mother:
Bind them continually upon thine
heart, and tie them about thy neck.
PROVERBS 6:20-21

*L*o, children are an heritage of the LORD:
and the fruit of the womb is his reward.
As arrows are in the hand of a mighty
man; so are children of the youth.
Happy is the man that hath
his quiver full of them.
PSALM 127:3-5

Not as though I wrote a new
commandment unto thee, but that
which we had from the beginning,
that we love one another.
2 John 5

But as for me and my house,
we will serve the Lord.
Joshua 24:15

Now ye are the body of Christ,
and members in particular.
1 Corinthians 12:27

Having predestinated us unto
the adoption of children by
Jesus Christ to himself,
according to the good pleasure
of his will.
Ephesians 1:5

Forgiveness

Come now, and let us reason together, saith the LORD: though your sins be as scarlet, they shall be as white as snow; though they be red like crimson, they shall be as wool.
ISAIAH 1:18

To the Lord our God belong mercies and forgivenesses.
DANIEL 9:9

If we confess our sins, he is faithful and just to forgive us our sins, and to cleanse us from all unrighteousness.
1 JOHN 1:9

And when ye stand praying, forgive, if ye have ought against any: that your Father also which is in heaven may forgive you your trespasses.
MARK 11:25

Be ye therefore merciful, as your
Father also is merciful. Judge not,
and ye shall not be judged: condemn
not, and ye shall not be condemned:
forgive, and ye shall be forgiven.
LUKE 6:36-37

Not by works of righteousness which we
have done, but according to his mercy he
saved us, by the washing of regeneration,
and renewing of the Holy Ghost.
TITUS 3:5

Who hath delivered us from the power
of darkness, and hath translated us
into the kingdom of his dear Son: in
whom we have redemption through his
blood, even the forgiveness of sins.
COLOSSIANS 1:13-14

For if ye forgive men their trespasses,
your heavenly Father will also forgive you.
MATTHEW 6:14

As far as the east is from the
west, so far hath he removed
our transgressions from us.
PSALM 103:12

Son, be of good cheer; thy
sins be forgiven thee.
MATTHEW 9:2

Blessed are they whose iniquities
are forgiven, and whose sins are covered.
ROMANS 4:7

If my people, which are called by
my name, shall humble themselves,
and pray, and seek my face, and turn
from their wicked ways; then will I
hear from heaven, and will forgive
their sin, and will heal their land.
2 CHRONICLES 7:14

And you, being dead in your sins and
the uncircumcision of your flesh, hath
he quickened together with him, having
forgiven you all trespasses; blotting out
the handwriting of ordinances that was
against us, which was contrary to us, and
took it out of the way, nailing it to his cross.
COLOSSIANS 2:13-14

I, even I, am he that blotteth out thy
transgressions for mine own sake,
and will not remember thy sins.
ISAIAH 43:25

Friendship

Two are better than one; because
they have a good reward for
their labour. For if they fall,
the one will lift up his fellow.
ECCLESIASTES 4:9-10

A new commandment
I give unto you,
that ye love one another;
as I have loved
you, that ye also
love one another.
By this shall all men know
that ye are my disciples,
if ye have love one to another.
JOHN 13:34-35

Ointment and perfume rejoice the
heart: so doth the sweetness of a
man's friend by hearty counsel.
PROVERBS 27:9

For where two or three are
gathered together in my name,
there am I in the midst of them.
MATTHEW 18:20

Let nothing be done through
strife or vainglory; but in lowliness
of mind let each esteem other better
than themselves. Look not every
man on his own things, but every
man also on the things of others.
PHILIPPIANS 2:3-4

Iron sharpeneth iron;
so a man sharpeneth the
countenance of his friend.
PROVERBS 27:17

Beloved, let us love one another:
for love is of God; and every one that
loveth is born of God, and knoweth God.
1 JOHN 4:7

*G*reater love hath no man than this, that
a man lay down his life for his friends.
JOHN 15:13

A friend loveth at all times, and
a brother is born for adversity.
PROVERBS 17:17

*B*ear ye one another's burdens,
and so fulfil the law of Christ.
GALATIANS 6:2

*T*he liberal soul shall be made fat.
PROVERBS 11:25

*A*nd as ye would that men should do
to you, do ye also to them likewise.
LUKE 6:31

Future

There are many devices in a man's heart; nevertheless the counsel of the Lord, that shall stand.
PROVERBS 19:21

Take therefore no thought for the morrow: for the morrow shall take thought for the things of itself. Sufficient unto the day is the evil thereof.
MATTHEW 6:34

In thy book all my members were written, which in continuance were fashioned, when as yet there was none of them.
PSALM 139:16

Grant thee according to thine own heart, and fulfil all thy counsel.
PSALM 20:4

Eye hath not seen, nor ear heard,
neither have entered into the heart
of man, the things which God hath
prepared for them that love him.
1 CORINTHIANS 2:9

For the LORD thy God, he it is
that doth go with thee; he will not
fail thee, nor forsake thee.
DEUTERONOMY 31:6

For I know the thoughts that I
think toward you, saith the LORD,
thoughts of peace, and not of evil,
to give you an expected end.
JEREMIAH 29:11

Teach me thy way, O LORD;
I will walk in thy truth.
PSALM 86:11

I therefore, the prisoner of the Lord,
beseech you that ye walk worthy of the
vocation wherewith ye are called.
EPHESIANS 4:1

The LORD will perfect that
which concerneth me: thy mercy,
O LORD, endureth for ever.
PSALM 138:8

According to my earnest expectation
and my hope, that in nothing I
shall be ashamed, but that with all
boldness, as always, so now also Christ
shall be magnified in my body.
PHILIPPIANS 1:20

O lord, thou hast searched me, and
known me. Thou knowest my downsitting
and mine uprising, thou understandest
my thought afar off. Thou compassest
my path and my lying down, and
art acquainted with all my ways.
PSALM 139:1-3

If then God so clothe the grass, which
is to day in the field, and to morrow is
cast into the oven; how much more will
he clothe you, O ye of little faith?
LUKE 12:28

Generosity

Give, and it shall be given unto you;
good measure, pressed down, and
shaken together, and running over, shall
men give into your bosom. For with
the same measure that ye mete withal
it shall be measured to you again.
LUKE 6:38

Every man according as he
purposeth in his heart, so let him
give; not grudgingly, or of necessity:
for God loveth a cheerful giver.
2 CORINTHIANS 9:7

Use hospitality one to another without
grudging. As every man hath received
the gift, even so minister the same
one to another, as good stewards
of the manifold grace of God.
1 PETER 4:9-10

Verily I say unto you, Inasmuch as ye
have done it unto one of the least of these
my brethren, ye have done it unto me.
MATTHEW 25:40

Whatsoever ye do, do it heartily,
as to the Lord, and not unto men.
COLOSSIANS 3:23

There is that withholdeth
more than is meet.
PROVERBS 11:24

Trust in the living God, who giveth
us richly all things to enjoy.
1 TIMOTHY 6:17

For ye know the grace of our
Lord Jesus Christ, that,
though he was rich, yet for your
sakes he became poor, that ye
through his poverty might be rich.
2 CORINTHIANS 8:9

He that hath a bountiful eye
shall be blessed; for he giveth
of his bread to the poor.
PROVERBS 22:9

Therefore take no thought, saying,
What shall we eat? or, What shall we
drink? or, Wherewithal shall we be
clothed? (For after all these things do the
Gentiles seek:) for your heavenly Father
knoweth that ye have need of all these
things. But seek ye first the kingdom
of God, and his righteousness; and all
these things shall be added unto you.
MATTHEW 6:31-33

Freely ye have received, freely give.
MATTHEW 10:8

Many, O LORD my God, are thy
wonderful works which thou hast done,
and thy thoughts which are to us-ward:
they cannot be reckoned up in
order unto thee: if I would declare
and speak of them, they are more
than can be numbered.
PSALM 40:5

God's Goodness

*O*h how great is thy goodness, which
thou hast laid up for them that fear thee;
which thou hast wrought for them that
trust in thee before the sons of men!
PSALM 31:19

*A*nd, behold, one came and said unto
him, Good Master, what good thing
shall I do, that I may have eternal life?
and he said unto him, Why callest
thou me good? there is none good but
one, that is, God: but if thou wilt enter
into life, keep the commandments.
MATTHEW 19:16-17

*G*ood and upright is the LORD:
therefore will he teach sinners in the way.
PSALM 25:8

O my soul, thou hast said unto
the LORD, thou art my Lord: my
goodness extendeth not to thee.
PSALM 16:2

O Lord, how manifold are thy works!
in wisdom hast thou made them all:
the earth is full of thy riches.
Psalm 104:24

I have trusted in thy mercy;
my heart shall rejoice in thy salvation.
I will sing unto the Lord, because he
hath dealt bountifully with me.
Psalm 13:5-6

The Lord is good, a strong hold in
the day of trouble; and he knoweth
them that trust in him.
Nahum 1:7

O give thanks unto the Lord; for he is
good; for his mercy endureth for ever.
1 Chronicles 16:34

Praise the Lord of hosts:
for the Lord is good; for his
mercy endureth for ever.
Jeremiah 33:11

According as his divine power hath
given unto us all things that pertain
unto life and godliness, through
the knowledge of him that hath
called us to glory and virtue.
2 PETER 1:3

Oh that men would praise the LORD
for his goodness, and for his wonderful
works to the children of men! For he
satisfieth the longing soul, and filleth
the hungry soul with goodness.
PSALM 107:8-9

And he will love thee, and bless thee.
DEUTERONOMY 7:13

Through the tender mercy of
our God; whereby the dayspring
from on high hath visited us.
LUKE 1:78

And of his fulness have all we
received, and grace for grace.
JOHN 1:16

May you know the love of Christ,
which passeth knowledge,
that ye might be filled with
all the fulness of God.
EPHESIANS 3:19

Every good gift and every perfect gift
is from above, and cometh down from
the Father of lights, with whom is no
variableness, neither shadow of turning.
JAMES 1:17

Knowing that whatsoever good
thing any man doeth, the same
shall he receive of the Lord.
EPHESIANS 6:8

God thundereth marvellously with
his voice; great things doeth he,
which we cannot comprehend.
JOB 37:5

God's Presence

For he hath said, I will never
leave thee, nor forsake thee.
HEBREWS 13:5

Lo, I am with you always, even
unto the end of the world.
MATTHEW 28:20

Behold, I stand at the door,
and knock: if any man hear my voice,
and open the door, I will come in to him,
and will sup with him, and he with me.
REVELATION 3:20

Draw nigh to God, and he
will draw nigh to you.
JAMES 4:8

The LORD is nigh unto all them that call upon him, to all that call upon him in truth. He will fulfil the desire of them that fear him: he also will hear their cry, and will save them.
PSALM 145:18-19

For, behold, the kingdom of God is within you.
LUKE 17:21

Be strong and of a good courage; be not afraid, neither be thou dismayed: for the LORD thy God is with thee whithersoever thou goest.
JOSHUA 1:9

And the LORD, he it is that doth go before thee; he will be with thee, he will not fail thee, neither forsake thee: fear not, neither be dismayed.
DEUTERONOMY 31:8

God himself is with us for our captain.
2 CHRONICLES 13:12

O have set the LORD always before
me: because he is at my right
hand, I shall not be moved.
PSALM 16:8

The hand of our God is upon all
them for good that seek him.
EZRA 8:22

Christ Jesus our Lord: in whom
we have boldness and access with
confidence by the faith of him.
EPHESIANS 3:11-12

God is in the generation of the righteous.
PSALM 14:5

For thou hast been a shelter for me,
and a strong tower from the enemy.
PSALM 61:3

The LORD is with you, while ye
be with him; and if ye seek him,
he will be found of you.
1 CHRONICLES 15:2

And even to your old age I am he;
and even to hoar hairs will I carry
you: I have made, and I will bear; even
I will carry, and will deliver you.
ISAIAH 46:4

I will both lay me down in peace,
and sleep: for thou, LORD, only
makest me dwell in safety.
PSALM 4:8

The LORD is my rock, and my fortress,
and my deliverer; my God, my strength,
in whom I will trust; my buckler.
PSALM 18:2

And ye shall seek me, and find me, when
ye shall search for me with all your heart.
JEREMIAH 29:13

My presence shall go with thee,
and I will give thee rest.
EXODUS 33:14

God's Provision

The LORD is my shepherd; I shall not want.
PSALM 23:1

Take no thought for your life, what
ye shall eat, or what ye shall drink;
nor yet for your body, what ye shall
put on. Is not the life more than
meat, and the body than raiment?
MATTHEW 6:25

But my God shall supply all
your need according to his riches
in glory by Christ Jesus.
PHILIPPIANS 4:19

Be not ye therefore like unto them:
for your Father knoweth what things
ye have need of, before ye ask him.
MATTHEW 6:8

He causeth the grass to grow
for the cattle, and herb for the
service of man: that he may bring
forth food out of the earth.
PSALM 104:14

God is able to make all grace abound
toward you; that ye, always having
all sufficiency in all things, may
abound to every good work.
2 CORINTHIANS 9:8

Let us not be weary in well doing: for in
due season we shall reap, if we faint not.
GALATIANS 6:9

Wherefore, if God so clothe the grass of
the field, which to day is, and to morrow
is cast into the oven, shall he not much
more clothe you, O ye of little faith?
MATTHEW 6:30

God's Word

The grass withereth,
the flower fadeth: but the word of
our God shall stand for ever.
ISAIAH 40:8

Thy word is a lamp unto my feet,
and a light unto my path.
PSALM 119:105

If a man love me, he will keep
my words: and my Father will love
him, and we will come unto him,
and make our abode with him.
JOHN 14:23

Yea rather, blessed are they that
hear the word of God, and keep it.
LUKE 11:28

Then said Jesus to those Jews which
believed on him, If ye continue in
my word, then are ye my disciples
indeed; and ye shall know the truth,
and the truth shall make you free.
JOHN 8:31-32

But be ye doers of the word,
and not hearers only.
JAMES 1:22

Great peace have they which love
thy law: and nothing shall offend them.
PSALM 119:165

His Son who being the brightness
of his glory, and the express image
of his person, and upholding all
things by the word of his power.
HEBREWS 1:3

As for God, his way is perfect:
the word of the LORD is tried: he is a
buckler to all those that trust in him.
PSALM 18:30

I know that his commandment
is life everlasting: whatsoever I
speak therefore, even as the Father
said unto me, so I speak.
JOHN 12:50

For the word of the LORD is right;
and all his works are done in truth.
PSALM 33:4

God's Word

Thy words were found,
and I did eat them; and thy word
was unto me the joy and rejoicing
of mine heart: for I am called by
thy name, O LORD God of hosts.
JEREMIAH 15:16

By the word of God the heavens
were of old, and the earth standing
out of the water and in the water.
2 PETER 3:5

But whoso keepeth his word, in him
verily is the love of God perfected:
hereby know we that we are in him.
1 JOHN 2:5

This book of the law shall not depart out
of thy mouth; but thou shalt meditate
therein day and night, that thou
mayest observe to do according to all
that is written therein: for then thou
shalt make thy way prosperous, and
then thou shalt have good success.
JOSHUA 1:8

Heaven and earth shall pass away,
but my words shall not pass away.
MATTHEW 24:35

Grace

God is able to make all grace abound
toward you; that ye, always having
all sufficiency in all things, may
abound to every good work.
2 CORINTHIANS 9:8

The grace of the Lord Jesus Christ, and
the love of God, and the communion
of the Holy Ghost, be with you all.
2 CORINTHIANS 13:14

For by grace are ye saved through
faith; and that not of yourselves: it
is the gift of God: not of works, lest
any man should boast. For we are his
workmanship, created in Christ Jesus
unto good works, which God hath before
ordained that we should walk in them.
EPHESIANS 2:8-10

We believe that through
the grace of the Lord Jesus
Christ we shall be saved.
ACTS 15:11

For ye know the grace of our Lord
Jesus Christ, that, though he was rich,
yet for your sakes he became poor, that
ye through his poverty might be rich.
2 CORINTHIANS 8:9

My grace is sufficient for thee: for my
strength is made perfect in weakness.
2 CORINTHIANS 12:9

God giveth grace unto the humble.
JAMES 4:6

God who hath saved us,
and called us with an holy calling,
not according to our works,
but according to his own purpose
and grace, which was given us in
Christ Jesus before the world began.
2 TIMOTHY 1:9

Therefore being justified by faith,
we have peace with God through
our Lord Jesus Christ: by whom also
we have access by faith into this
grace wherein we stand, and rejoice
in hope of the glory of God.
ROMANS 5:1-2

Let us therefore come boldly
unto the throne of grace, that
we may obtain mercy, and find
grace to help in time of need.
HEBREWS 4:16

In whom [Christ] we have redemption
through his blood, the forgiveness of sins,
according to the riches of his grace.
EPHESIANS 1:7

But unto every one of us is
given grace according to the
measure of the gift of Christ.
EPHESIANS 4:7

Gratitude

The LORD is my strength and my shield;
my heart trusted in him, and I am helped:
therefore my heart greatly rejoiceth;
and with my song will I praise him.
PSALM 28:7

For every creature of God is good,
and nothing to be refused, if it be
received with thanksgiving.
1 TIMOTHY 4:4

My heart rejoiceth in the LORD,
mine horn is exalted in the LORD.
1 SAMUEL 2:1

The LORD hath done great things
for us; whereof we are glad.
PSALM 126:3

I will praise the Lord with my
whole heart, in the assembly of the
upright, and in the congregation.
The works of the Lord are great.
Psalm 111:1-2

*O*h that men would praise the
Lord for his goodness.
Psalm 107:31

I will praise thee, O Lord, with
my whole heart; I will shew forth
all thy marvellous works.
Psalm 9:1

*P*raise the Lord of hosts:
for the Lord is good.
Jeremiah 33:11

*T*hanks be unto God, which always
causeth us to triumph in Christ, and
maketh manifest the savour of his
knowledge by us in every place.
2 Corinthians 2:14

O give thanks unto the God of gods:
for his mercy endureth for ever.
PSALM 136:2

*I*n every thing give thanks:
for this is the will of God in
Christ Jesus concerning you.
1 THESSALONIANS 5:18

*S*trengthened with all might, according
to his glorious power, unto all patience
and longsuffering with joyfulness;
giving thanks unto the Father, which
hath made us meet to be partakers of
the inheritance of the saints in light.
COLOSSIANS 1:11-12

*T*he LORD hath done great things
for us; whereof we are glad.
PSALM 126:3

*U*nto thee, O God, do we
give thanks, unto thee do we
thanks: for that thy name is near
thy wondrous works declare.
PSALM 75:1

Guidance

I will instruct thee and teach thee
in the way which thou shalt go:
I will guide thee with mine eye.
PSALM 32:8

Shew me thy ways, O LORD;
teach me thy paths. Lead me in
thy truth, and teach me: for thou
art the God of my salvation; on
thee do I wait all the day.
PSALM 25:4-5

He leadeth me in the paths
of righteousness.
PSALM 23:3

Ye shall walk in all the ways
which the LORD your God hath
commanded you, that ye may live,
and that it may be well with you,
and that ye may prolong your days
in the land which ye shall possess.
DEUTERONOMY 5:33

The LORD on the head of them.
MICAH 2:13

Thou in thy mercy hast led forth the
people which thou hast redeemed:
thou hast guided them in thy
strength unto thy holy habitation.
EXODUS 15:13

Teach me to do thy will; for thou
art my God: thy spirit is good; lead
me into the land of uprightness.
PSALM 143:10

Enter into his gates with thanksgiving,
and into his courts with praise:
be thankful unto him, and bless his name.
PSALM 100:4

Thou hast made known to me the
ways of life; thou shalt make me
full of joy with thy countenance.
ACTS 2:28

For it is God which worketh in you both
to will and to do of his good pleasure.
PHILIPPIANS 2:13

I will bring the blind by a way that
they knew not; I will lead them in
paths that they have not known:
I will make darkness light before
them, and crooked things straight.
ISAIAH 42:16

In all thy ways acknowledge him,
and he shall direct thy paths.
PROVERBS 3:6

I am the vine, ye are the branches:
he that abideth in me, and I in him,
the same bringeth forth much fruit:
for without me ye can do nothing.
JOHN 15:5

Jesus saith unto him, I am the
way, the truth, and the life: no man
cometh unto the Father, but by me.
JOHN 14:6

Order my steps in thy word:
and let not any iniquity have
dominion over me.
PSALM 119:133

For as many as are led by the Spirit
of God, they are the sons of God.
ROMANS 8:14

Fear thou not; for I am with thee:
be not dismayed; for I am thy God:
I will strengthen thee;
yea, I will help thee.
ISAIAH 41:10

Holy Spirit

The fruit of the Spirit is love, joy, peace, longsuffering, gentleness, goodness, faith, meekness, temperance.
GALATIANS 5:22-23

The Comforter, which is the Holy Ghost, whom the Father will send in my name, he shall teach you all things, and bring all things to your remembrance, whatsoever I have said unto you.
JOHN 14:26

Likewise the Spirit also helpeth our infirmities: for we know not what we should pray for as we ought: but the Spirit itself maketh intercession for us with groanings which cannot be uttered.
ROMANS 8:26

Hope maketh not ashamed; because the love of God is shed abroad in our hearts by the Holy Ghost which is given unto us.
ROMANS 5:5

If we live in the Spirit,
let us also walk in the Spirit.
GALATIANS 5:25

For whatsoever a man soweth,
that shall he also reap. He that
soweth to the Spirit shall of
the Spirit reap life everlasting.
GALATIANS 6:7-8

When he, the Spirit of truth, is come,
he will guide you into all truth.
JOHN 16:13

We have received, not the spirit of
the world, but the spirit which is of
God; that we might know the things
that are freely given to us of God.
1 CORINTHIANS 2:12

Not by might, nor by power, but by
my spirit, saith the LORD of hosts.
ZECHARIAH 4:6

Know ye not that your body is the
temple of the Holy Ghost which is
in you, which ye have of God.
1 CORINTHIANS 6:19

*B*ut the anointing which ye have received of him abideth in you, and ye need not that any man teach you: but as the same anointing teacheth you of all things, and is truth.
1 JOHN 2:27

*B*ut ye, beloved, building up yourselves on your most holy faith, praying in the Holy Ghost.
JUDE 20

*F*or they that are after the flesh do mind the things of the flesh; but they that are after the Spirit the things of the Spirit. For to be carnally minded is death; but to be spiritually minded is life and peace.
ROMANS 8:5-6

Honesty

Every man shall kiss his lips
that giveth a right answer.
PROVERBS 24:26

Blessed is the man unto whom the
LORD imputeth not iniquity, and in
whose spirit there is no guile.
PSALM 32:2

O continue thy lovingkindness
unto them that know thee; and thy
righteousness to the upright in heart.
PSALM 36:10

Mark the perfect man, and behold the
upright: for the end of that man is peace.
PSALM 37:37

For I say to every man that is among
you, not to think of himself more highly
than he ought to think; but to think
soberly, according as God hath dealt
to every man the measure of faith.
ROMANS 12:3

All the paths of the LORD are mercy
and truth unto such as keep his
covenant and his testimonies.
PSALM 25:10

O send out thy light and thy truth:
let them lead me; let them bring me
unto thy holy hill, and to thy tabernacles.
PSALM 43:3

I have chosen the way of truth:
thy judgments have I laid before me.
PSALM 119:30

God is a Spirit: and they that
worship him must worship
him in spirit and in truth.
JOHN 4:24

Hope

But they that wait upon the LORD
shall renew their strength; they shall
mount up with wings as eagles;
they shall run, and not be weary;
and they shall walk, and not faint.
ISAIAH 40:31

Now the God of hope fill you
with all joy and peace in believing,
that ye may abound in hope, through
the power of the Holy Ghost.
ROMANS 15:13

For thou art my hope, O Lord God:
thou art my trust from my youth.
PSALM 71:5

Which hope we have as an anchor
of the soul, both sure and stedfast.
HEBREWS 6:19

Let thy mercy, O Lord, be upon us,
according as we hope in thee.
PSALM 33:22

For therefore we both labour and
suffer reproach, because we trust in
the living God, who is the Saviour of all
men, specially of those that believe.
1 TIMOTHY 4:10

The counsel of the LORD standeth
for ever, the thoughts of his
heart to all generations.
PSALM 33:11

And thou shalt be secure, because there
is hope; yea, thou shalt dig about thee,
and thou shalt take thy rest in safety.
JOB 11:18

The LORD is good unto them that wait
for him, to the soul that seeketh him.
LAMENTATIONS 3:25

Thou shalt know that I am the LORD: for
they shall not be ashamed that wait for me.
ISAIAH 49:23

Let us hold fast the profession of
our faith without wavering; (for
he is faithful that promised;).
HEBREWS 10:23

Yea, let none that wait on
thee be ashamed.
PSALM 25:3

In the multitude of my thoughts
within me thy comforts delight my soul.
PSALM 94:19

Humility

Humble yourselves therefore
under the mighty hand of God,
that he may exalt you in due time.
1 PETER 5:6

Blessed are the meek:
for they shall inherit the earth.
MATTHEW 5:5

By humility and the fear of the
LORD are riches, and honour, and life.
PROVERBS 22:4

The humble shall see this, and be glad:
and your heart shall live that seek God.
PSALM 69:32

The meek will he guide in judgment:
and the meek will he teach his way.
PSALM 25:9

The LORD lifteth up the meek.
PSALM 147:6

*P*ut on therefore, as the elect of
God, holy and beloved, bowels of
mercies, kindness, humbleness of
mind, meekness, longsuffering.
COLOSSIANS 3:12

*F*inally, be ye all of one mind,
having compassion one of another, love as
brethren, be pitiful, be courteous.
1 PETER 3:8

*W*ith all lowliness and meekness,
with longsuffering, forbearing
one another in love.
EPHESIANS 4:2

*F*or whosoever exalteth himself
shall be abased; and he that humbleth
himself shall be exalted.
LUKE 14:11

*F*or the LORD taketh pleasure
in his people: he will beautify
the meek with salvation.
PSALM 149:4

*H*umble yourselves in the sight of
the LORD, and he shall lift you up.
JAMES 4:10

Integrity

The just man walketh in his integrity:
his children are blessed after him.
PROVERBS 20:7

Let integrity and uprightness
preserve me; for I wait on thee.
PSALM 25:21

In your patience possess ye your souls.
LUKE 21:19

The integrity of the upright
shall guide them.
PROVERBS 11:3

And as for me, thou upholdest
me in mine integrity, and settest
me before thy face for ever.
PSALM 41:12

He layeth up sound wisdom for
the righteous: he is a buckler to
them that walk uprightly.
PROVERBS 2:7

Righteousness keepeth him
that is upright in the way.
PROVERBS 13:6

I know also, my God, that thou
triest the heart, and hast pleasure
in uprightness. As for me, in the
uprightness of mine heart I have
willingly offered all these things.
1 CHRONICLES 29:17

Blessed are the undefiled in the way,
who walk in the law of the LORD. Blessed
are they that keep his testimonies, and
that seek him with the whole heart.
PSALM 119:1-2

In doctrine shewing uncorruptness,
gravity, sincerity, sound speech,
that cannot be condemned.
TITUS 2:7-8

He that walketh uprightly
walketh surely.
PROVERBS 10:9

For the righteous LORD loveth
righteousness; his countenance
doth behold the upright.
PSALM 11:7

Jesus Christ

$\mathcal{I}$ am the bread of life: he that cometh
to me shall never hunger; and he that
believeth on me shall never thirst.
JOHN 6:35

$\mathcal{I}$ am come a light into the world,
that whosoever believeth on me
should not abide in darkness.
JOHN 12:46

$\mathcal{I}$ am the resurrection, and the life:
he that believeth in me, though he were
dead, yet shall he live: and whosoever
liveth and believeth in me shall never die.
JOHN 11:25-26

$\mathcal{I}$ am the way, the truth,
and the life: no man cometh
unto the Father, but by me.
JOHN 14:6

But if we walk in the light,
as he is in the light, we have
fellowship one with another,
and the blood of Jesus Christ
his Son cleanseth us from all sin.
1 JOHN 1:7

Wherefore God also hath highly
exalted him, and given him
a name which is above every name:
that at the name of Jesus every knee
should bow, of things in heaven,
and things in earth, and things under
the earth; and that every tongue
should confess that Jesus Christ is
Lord, to the glory of God the Father.
PHILIPPIANS 2:9-11

God hath given to us eternal life,
and this life is in his Son. He that
hath the Son hath life; and he that
hath not the Son of God hath not life.
1 JOHN 5:11-12

I am the good shepherd,
and know my sheep, and am known
of mine. As the Father knoweth me,
even so know I the Father:
and I lay down my life for the sheep.
JOHN 10:14-15

*B*ut now in Christ Jesus ye who
sometimes were far off are made
nigh by the blood of Christ.
EPHESIANS 2:13

*T*herefore if any man be in Christ,
he is a new creature: old things
are passed away; behold,
all things are become new.
2 CORINTHIANS 5:17

*H*e is the propitiation for our sins:
and not for ours only, but also for
the sins of the whole world.
1 JOHN 2:2

Joy

This is the day which the LORD hath
made; we will rejoice and be glad in it.
PSALM 118:24

Enter into his gates with thanksgiving,
and into his courts with praise:
be thankful unto him, and bless
his name. For the LORD is good;
his mercy is everlasting; and his
truth endureth to all generations.
PSALM 100:4-5

These things have I spoken unto you,
that my joy might remain in you,
and that your joy might be full.
JOHN 15:11

The joy of the LORD is your strength.
NEHEMIAH 8:10

Rejoice, because your names
are written in heaven.
LUKE 10:20

Thou wilt shew me the path of life:
in thy presence is fulness of
joy; at thy right hand there
are pleasures for evermore.
PSALM 16:11

Happy is that people,
whose God is the LORD.
PSALM 144:15

A merry heart maketh a
cheerful countenance.
PROVERBS 15:13

O give thanks unto the LORD, for he is
good: for his mercy endureth for ever.
PSALM 107:1

For thou, LORD, hast made me glad
through thy work: I will triumph
in the works of thy hands.
PSALM 92:4

Glory ye in his holy name:
let the heart of them rejoice
that seek the LORD.
1 CHRONICLES 16:10

*L*ight is sown for the righteous,
and gladness for the upright in heart.
PSALM 97:11

*F*or our heart shall rejoice in him,
because we have trusted in his holy name.
PSALM 33:21

*G*lory ye in his holy name: let the heart
of them rejoice that seek the LORD.
PSALM 105:3

I will greatly rejoice in the LORD,
my soul shall be joyful in my God;
for he hath clothed me with the
garments of salvation, he hath covered
me with the robe of righteousness.
ISAIAH 61:10

*R*ejoice evermore.
1 THESSALONIANS 5:16

Justice

He hath shewed thee, O man, what is good; and what doth the LORD require of thee, but to do justly, and to love mercy, and to walk humbly with thy God?
MICAH 6:8

Yea, surely God will not do wickedly, neither will the Almighty pervert judgment.
JOB 34:12

A just weight and balance are the LORD's: all the weights of the bag are his work.
PROVERBS 16:11

Keep mercy and judgment and wait on thy God continually.
HOSEA 12:6

The law of the LORD is perfect, converting the soul.
PSALM 19:7

The Almighty ... is excellent
in power, and in judgment,
and in plenty of justice.
JOB 37:23

Blessed are they that keep
judgment, and he that doeth
righteousness at all times.
PSALM 106:3

Great and marvellous are thy works,
Lord God Almighty; just and true
are thy ways, thou King of saints.
REVELATION 15:3

He is the LORD our God; his
judgments are in all the earth.
1 CHRONICLES 16:14

O LORD, when I plead with thee:
yet let me talk with thee of thy judgments.
JEREMIAH 12:1

For the righteous LORD loveth
righteousness; his countenance
doth behold the upright.
PSALM 11:7

That which is altogether just shalt
thou follow, that thou mayest live,
and inherit the land which the
Lord thy God giveth thee.
DEUTERONOMY 16:20

Learn to do well; seek judgment,
relieve the oppressed, judge the
fatherless, plead for the widow.
ISAIAH 1:17

Let judgment run down as waters,
and righteousness as a mighty stream.
AMOS 5:24

For the Lord will not cast off
his people, neither will he forsake
his inheritance. But judgment shall
return unto righteousness: and all
the upright in heart shall follow it.
PSALM 94:14-15

Kindness

$\mathcal{F}$or we are his workmanship, created
in Christ Jesus unto good works,
which God hath before ordained
that we should walk in them.
EPHESIANS 2:10

$\mathcal{I}$f any man minister, let him do it
as of the ability which God giveth:
that God in all things may be
glorified through Jesus Christ,
to whom be praise and
dominion for ever and ever.
1 PETER 4:11

$\mathcal{H}$e that hath pity upon the poor
lendeth unto the LORD; and that which
he hath given will he pay him again.
PROVERBS 19:17

$\mathcal{A}$nd be ye kind one to another,
tenderhearted, forgiving
one another, even as God for
Christ's sake hath forgiven you.
EPHESIANS 4:32

As we have therefore opportunity,
let us do good unto all men,
especially unto them who are
of the household of faith.
GALATIANS 6:10

Be perfect, be of good comfort, be of
one mind, live in peace; and the God
of love and peace shall be with you.
2 CORINTHIANS 13:11

Ye should be married to another,
even to him who is raised from
the dead, that we should bring
forth fruit unto God.
ROMANS 7:4

Gracious is the LORD, and righteous;
yea, our God is merciful.
PSALM 116:5

The merciful man doeth
good to his own soul.
PROVERBS 11:17

Therefore all things whatsoever
ye would that men should do to
you, do ye even so to them.
MATTHEW 7:12

He that honoureth him
hath mercy on the poor.
PROVERBS 14:31

For his merciful kindness is great
toward us: and the truth of the LORD
endureth for ever. Praise ye the LORD.
PSALM 117:2

O give thanks unto the LORD; for he is
good: because his mercy endureth for ever.
PSALM 118:1

But after that the kindness and
love of God our Saviour toward
man appeared, not by works of
righteousness which we have done,
but according to his mercy he saved us.
TITUS 3:4-5

Be not weary in well doing.
2 THESSALONIANS 3:13

love

$\mathcal{B}$ehold, what manner of love the
Father hath bestowed upon us, that
we should be called the sons of God.
1 JOHN 3:1

$\mathcal{F}$or I am persuaded, that neither death,
nor life, nor angels, nor principalities,
nor powers, nor things present, nor
things to come, nor height, nor depth,
nor any other creature, shall be able
to separate us from the love of God,
which is in Christ Jesus our Lord.
ROMANS 8:38-39

$\mathcal{O}$ satisfy us early with thy mercy; that
we may rejoice and be glad all our days.
PSALM 90:14

Thou shalt love thy neighbour as thyself.
Love worketh no ill to his neighbour:
therefore love is the fulfilling of the law.
ROMANS 13:9-10

But whoso keepeth his word, in him
verily is the love of God perfected.
1 JOHN 2:5

Hereby perceive we the love of
God, because he laid down his life
for us: and we ought to lay down
our lives for the brethren.
1 JOHN 3:16

To him who alone doeth great wonders:
for his mercy endureth for ever.
PSALM 136:4

Above all things have fervent
charity among yourselves: for charity
shall cover the multitude of sins.
1 PETER 4:8

For I have said, Mercy shall be built up for ever: thy faithfulness shalt thou establish in the very heavens.
PSALM 89:2

Grace be with you, mercy, and peace, from God the Father, and from the Lord Jesus Christ, the Son of the Father, in truth and love.
2 JOHN 1:3

If we love one another, God dwelleth in us, and his love is perfected in us.
1 JOHN 4:12

Love one another; as I have loved you, that ye also love one another.
JOHN 13:34

The mercy of the LORD is from everlasting to everlasting upon them that fear him, and his righteousness unto children's children.
PSALM 103:17

God commendeth his love toward
us, in that, while we were yet
sinners, Christ died for us.
ROMANS 5:8

The Lord which executeth judgment for
the oppressed: which giveth food to the
hungry. The LORD looseth the prisoners:
the LORD openeth the eyes of the blind:
the LORD raiseth them that are bowed
down: the LORD loveth the righteous.
PSALM 146:7-8

For all the law is fulfilled in one
word, even in this; Thou shalt
love thy neighbour as thyself.
GALATIANS 5:14

Beloved, let us love one another: for love
is of God; and every one that loveth is born
of God, and knoweth God. He that loveth
not knoweth not God; for God is love.
1 JOHN 4:7-8

Patience

The Lord is not slack concerning his
promise, as some men count slackness;
but is longsuffering to us-ward.
2 PETER 3:9

The LORD is longsuffering,
and of great mercy, forgiving
iniquity and transgression.
NUMBERS 14:18

Preach the word;
be instant in season,
out of season; reprove,
rebuke, exhort with all
long suffering and doctrine.
2 TIMOTHY 4:2

By long forbearing is
a prince persuaded.
PROVERBS 25:15

Better is the end of a thing
than the beginning thereof:
and the patient in spirit is
better than the proud in spirit.
ECCLESIASTES 7:8

Or despisest thou the riches of
his goodness and forbearance
and longsuffering; not knowing
that the goodness of God leadeth
thee to repentance?
ROMANS 2:4

Be ye also patient; stablish your hearts:
for the coming of the Lord draweth nigh.
JAMES 5:8

I waited patiently for the LORD; and he
inclined unto me, and heard my cry.
PSALM 40:1

Rest in the LORD, and wait
patiently for him.
PSALM 37:7

Rejoicing in hope;
patient in tribulation;
continuing instant in prayer.
ROMANS 12:12

Account that the longsuffering
of our Lord is salvation.
2 PETER 3:15

For ye have need of patience, that,
after ye have done the will of God,
ye might receive the promise.
HEBREWS 10:36

With all lowliness and meekness,
with longsuffering, forbearing
one another in love; endeavouring
to keep the unity of the Spirit
in the bond of peace.
EPHESIANS 4:2-3

We glory in tribulations also:
knowing that tribulation worketh
patience; and patience, experience;
and experience, hope.
ROMANS 5:3-4

Peace

$\mathcal{P}$eace I leave with you, my peace I give unto you: not as the world giveth, give I unto you. Let not your heart be troubled, neither let it be afraid.
JOHN 14:27

$\mathcal{T}$he peace of God, which passeth all understanding, shall keep your hearts and minds through Christ Jesus.
PHILIPPIANS 4:7

$\mathcal{T}$he LORD will give strength unto his people; the LORD will bless his people with peace.
PSALM 29:11

$\mathcal{T}$hou wilt keep him in perfect peace, whose mind is stayed on thee: because he trusteth in thee.
ISAIAH 26:3

*L*et the peace of God rule in your hearts, to the which also ye are called in one body; and be ye thankful.
COLOSSIANS 3:15

*C*ome unto me, all ye that labour and are heavy laden, and I will give you rest. Take my yoke upon you, and learn of me; for I am meek and lowly in heart: and ye shall find rest unto your souls. For my yoke is easy, and my burden is light.
MATTHEW 11:28-30

*T*here remaineth therefore a rest to the people of God. For he that is entered into his rest, he also hath ceased from his own works, as God did from his. Let us labour therefore to enter into that rest.
HEBREWS 4:9-11

*T*he very God of peace sanctify you wholly.
1 THESSALONIANS 5:23

Now the Lord of peace himself
give you peace always by all means.
The Lord be with you all.
2 Thessalonians 3:16

Mark the perfect man, and behold the
upright: for the end of that man is peace.
Psalm 37:37

Through the tender mercy of our God;
whereby the dayspring from on high
hath visited us, to give light to them
that sit in darkness and in the
shadow of death, to guide our
feet into the way of peace.
Luke 1:78-79

The Lord bless thee, and keep thee:
the Lord make his face shine upon
thee, and be gracious unto thee:
the Lord lift up his countenance
upon thee, and give thee peace.
Numbers 6:24-26

Perseverance

For we are saved by hope: but hope
that is seen is not hope: for what a man
seeth, why doth he yet hope for? But
if we hope for that we see not, then
do we with patience wait for it.
ROMANS 8:24-25

Let us not be weary in well doing:
for in due season we shall
reap, if we faint not.
GALATIANS 6:9

For ye have need of patience, that,
after ye have done the will of God,
ye might receive the promise.
HEBREWS 10:36

But he that shall endure unto
the end, the same shall be saved.
MATTHEW 24:13

Blessed are they which do hunger
and thirst after righteousness:
for they shall be filled.
MATTHEW 5:6

Blessed is the man that endureth
temptation: for when he is tried, he shall
receive the crown of life, which the Lord
hath promised to them that love him.
JAMES 1:12

Abide in me, and I in you.
JOHN 15:4

I follow after, if that I may
apprehend that for which also I am
apprehended of Christ Jesus.
PHILIPPIANS 3:12

Let patience have her perfect work,
that ye may be perfect and entire.
JAMES 1:4

But this one thing I do, forgetting those things which are behind, and reaching forth unto those things which are before, I press toward the mark for the prize of the high calling of God in Christ Jesus.
PHILIPPIANS 3:13-14

Giving all diligence, add to your faith virtue.
2 PETER 1:5

Now the God of patience and consolation grant you to be likeminded one toward another according to Christ Jesus.
ROMANS 15:5

The Lord direct your hearts into the love of God, and into the patient waiting for Christ.
2 THESSALONIANS 3:5

Be ye strong therefore, and let
not your hands be weak: for your
work shall be rewarded.
2 CHRONICLES 15:7

For which cause we faint not; but though
our outward man perish, yet the inward
man is renewed day by day. For our light
affliction, which is but for a moment,
worketh for us a far more exceeding and
eternal weight of glory; while we look not
at the things which are seen, but at the
things which are not seen: for the things
which are seen are temporal; but the
things which are not seen are eternal.
2 CORINTHIANS 4:16-18

For I reckon that the sufferings
of this present time are not worthy
to be compared with the glory
which shall be revealed in us.
ROMANS 8:18

Therefore, my beloved brethren,
be ye stedfast, unmoveable, always
abounding in the work of the Lord,
forasmuch as ye know that your
labour is not in vain in the Lord.
1 CORINTHIANS 15:58

Praise

O Lord, thou art my God; I will exalt
thee, I will praise thy name; for
thou hast done wonderful things.
Isaiah 25:1

Blessed is the people that know
the joyful sound: they shall walk,
O Lord, in the light of thy countenance.
In thy name shall they rejoice all
the day: and in thy righteousness
shall they be exalted.
Psalm 89:15-16

Because thy lovingkindness is better
than life, my lips shall praise thee.
Thus will I bless thee while I live: I
will lift up my hands in thy name.
Psalm 63:3-4

Glory to God in the highest, and on
earth peace, good will toward men.
Luke 2:14

It is a good thing to give thanks unto
the Lord, and to sing praises unto
thy name, O Most High: to shew forth
thy lovingkindness in the morning,
and thy faithfulness every night.
Psalm 92:1-2

Let your light so shine before men,
that they may see your good works, and
glorify your Father which is in heaven.
Matthew 5:16

Now unto him that is able to do
exceeding abundantly above all
that we ask or think, according to
the power that worketh in us.
Ephesians 3:20

Wherefore we receiving a kingdom which
cannot be moved, let us have grace,
whereby we may serve God acceptably
with reverence and godly fear.
Hebrews 12:28

Give thanks unto the LORD, call
upon his name, make known his
deeds among the people.
1 CHRONICLES 16:8

The LORD liveth; and blessed be my rock;
and let the God of my salvation be exalted.
PSALM 18:46

Give unto the LORD the glory due
unto his name; worship the LORD
in the beauty of holiness.
PSALM 29:2

I will praise thee; for I am
fearfully and wonderfully made:
marvellous are thy works; and that
my soul knoweth right well.
PSALM 139:14

Prayer

And this is the confidence that we
have in him, that, if we ask any thing
according to his will, he heareth us:
and if we know that he hear us,
whatsoever we ask, we know that we
have the petitions that we desired of him.
1 John 5:14-15

Ask, and it shall be given you; seek,
and ye shall find; knock,
and it shall be opened unto you:
for every one that asketh receiveth;
and he that seeketh findeth;
and to him that knocketh
it shall be opened.
Matthew 7:7-8

My prayer is unto thee, O Lord,
in an acceptable time: O God,
in the multitude of thy mercy hear
me, in the truth of thy salvation.
Psalm 69:13

Know that the LORD hath set apart
him that is godly for himself: the LORD
will hear when I call unto him.
PSALM 4:3

But thou, when thou prayest, enter
into thy closet, and when thou hast shut
thy door, pray to thy Father which is
in secret; and thy Father which seeth
in secret shall reward thee openly.
MATTHEW 6:6

Call unto me, and I will answer thee,
and show thee great and mighty
things, which thou knowest not.
JEREMIAH 33:3

I love the LORD, because he hath heard
my voice and my supplications. Because he
hath inclined his ear unto me, therefore
will I call upon him as long as I live.
PSALM 116:1-2

Rejoice evermore. Pray without ceasing.
In every thing give thanks: for this is the
will of God in Christ Jesus concerning you.
1 Thessalonians 5:16-18

Thou drewest near in the day that I
called upon thee: thou saidst, Fear not.
Lamentations 3:57

If any man be a worshipper of God,
and doeth his will, him he heareth.
John 9:31

Seek the Lord and his strength,
seek his face continually.
1 Chronicles 16:11

Confess your faults one to another, and pray one for another, that ye may be healed. The effectual fervent prayer of a righteous man availeth much.
JAMES 5:16

If two of you shall agree on earth as touching any thing that they shall ask, it shall be done for them of my Father which is in heaven. For where two or three are gathered together in my name, there am I in the midst of them.
MATTHEW 18:19-20

Hitherto have ye asked nothing in my name: ask, and ye shall receive, that your joy may be full.
JOHN 16:24

If ye abide in me, and my words abide in you, ye shall ask what ye will, and it shall be done unto you.
JOHN 15:7

Prosperity

But seek ye first the kingdom of God,
and his righteousness; and all these
things shall be added unto you.
MATTHEW 6:33

We know that all things work together
for good to them that love God,
to them who are the called
according to his purpose.
ROMANS 8:28

Let the beauty of the LORD our God
be upon us: and establish thou the
work of our hands upon us; yea, the
work of our hands establish thou it.
PSALM 90:17

If they obey and serve him, they
shall spend their days in prosperity,
and their years in pleasures.
JOB 36:11

For I know the thoughts that I
think toward you, saith the Lord,
thoughts of peace, and not of evil,
to give you an expected end.
JEREMIAH 29:11

God be merciful unto us, and bless us;
and cause his face to shine upon us.
PSALM 67:1

Then shalt thou prosper,
if thou takest heed to fulfil
the statutes and judgments which
the LORD charged Moses with.
1 CHRONICLES 22:13

Be ye stedfast, unmoveable, always
abounding in the work of the Lord,
forasmuch as ye know that your
labour is not in vain in the Lord.
1 CORINTHIANS 15:58

For unto every one that hath shall be
given, and he shall have abundance.
MATTHEW 25:29

The thoughts of the diligent
tend only to plenteousness.
PROVERBS 21:5

He that putteth his trust in
the LORD shall be made fat.
PROVERBS 28:25

The Lord who satisfieth thy mouth
with good things; so that thy youth
is renewed like the eagle's.
PSALM 103:5

Acquaint now thyself with him,
and be at peace: thereby good
shall come unto thee.
JOB 22:21

Reassurance

But this man, because he continueth ever, hath an unchangeable priesthood. Wherefore he is able also to save them to the uttermost that come unto God by him.
HEBREWS 7:24-25

For the eyes of the Lord are over the righteous, and his ears are open unto their prayers.
1 PETER 3:12

The LORD heareth the prayer of the righteous.
PROVERBS 15:29

He which hath begun a good work in you will perform it until the day of Jesus Christ.
PHILIPPIANS 1:6

I will never leave thee,
nor forsake thee.
HEBREWS 13:5

*F*or your Father knoweth what things
ye have need of, before ye ask him.
MATTHEW 6:8

*T*he LORD your God which goeth
before you, he shall fight for you.
DEUTERONOMY 1:30

*N*ay, in all these things we
are more than conquerors
through him that loved us.
ROMANS 8:37

*F*or I the LORD thy God will hold
thy right hand, saying unto thee,
Fear not; I will help thee.
ISAIAH 41:13

The eyes of the LORD are
upon the righteous.
PSALM 34:15

For surely there is an end; and thine
expectation shall not be cut off.
PROVERBS 23:18

For thus saith the high and lofty
One that inhabiteth eternity, whose
name is Holy; I dwell in the high and
holy place, with him also that is of a
contrite and humble spirit, to revive
the spirit of the humble, and to revive
the heart of the contrite ones.
ISAIAH 57:15

Whatsoever ye shall ask in prayer,
believing, ye shall receive.
MATTHEW 21:22

Reputation

Humble yourselves in the sight of
the Lord, and he shall lift you up.
JAMES 4:10

Let not mercy and truth forsake thee:
bind them about thy neck; write them
upon the table of thine heart: So shalt
thou find favour and good understanding
in the sight of God and man.
PROVERBS 3:3-4

For I say, through the grace given unto
me, to every man that is among you, not
to think of himself more highly than he
ought to think; but to think soberly.
ROMANS 12:3

I will praise thee for ever,
because thou hast done it: and I
will wait on thy name; for it
is good before thy saints.
PSALM 52:9

So didst thou get thee a
name, as it is this day.
NEHEMIAH 9:10

The cup of blessing which we bless, is it
not the communion of the blood of Christ?
The bread which we break, is it not the
communion of the body of Christ? For we
being many are one bread, and one body:
for we are all partakers of that one bread.
1 CORINTHIANS 10:16-17

Having your conversation
honest among the Gentiles: that,
whereas they speak against you as
evildoers, they may by your good
works, which they shall behold,
glorify God in the day of visitation.
1 PETER 2:12

For ye have not received the spirit
of bondage again to fear; but ye
have received the Spirit of adoption,
whereby we cry, Abba, Father.
ROMANS 8:15

For though I would desire to glory,
I shall not be a fool; for I will say the
truth: but now I forbear, lest any man
should think of me above that which he
seeth me to be, or that he heareth of me.
2 Corinthians 12:6

Giving all diligence, add to your faith
virtue; and to virtue knowledge; and to
knowledge temperance; and to temperance
patience; and to patience godliness;
and to godliness brotherly kindness;
and to brotherly kindness charity.
2 Peter 1:5-7

Keep therefore and do them [statutes
and judgments]; for this is your wisdom
and your understanding in the sight of
the nations, which shall hear all these
statutes, and say, Surely this great nation
is a wise and understanding people.
Deuteronomy 4:5-6

For I rejoiced greatly,
when the brethren came and testified
of the truth that is in thee, even
as thou walkest in the truth.
3 John 1:3

Rest

For I have satiated the weary soul, and
I have replenished every sorrowful soul.
JEREMIAH 31:25

Restore unto me the joy of thy salvation;
and uphold me with thy free spirit.
PSALM 51:12

Cast thy burden upon the LORD, and
he shall sustain thee: he shall never
suffer the righteous to be moved.
PSALM 55:22

My presence shall go with thee,
and I will give thee rest.
EXODUS 33:14

Truly my soul waiteth upon God:
from him cometh my salvation.
PSALM 62:1

My grace is sufficient for thee: for my
strength is made perfect in weakness.
2 CORINTHIANS 12:9

*C*ome unto me, all ye that labour and are
heavy laden, and I will give you rest.
MATTHEW 11:28

*F*or thus saith the LORD God,
the Holy One of Israel;
in returning and rest
shall ye be saved; in quietness
and in confidence shall be your strength.
ISAIAH 30:15

*T*he fear of the LORD tendeth to life:
and he that hath it shall abide satisfied;
he shall not be visited with evil.
PROVERBS 19:23

I laid me down and slept; I awaked;
for the Lord sustained me.
PSALM 3:5

Repent ye therefore, and be converted,
that your sins may be blotted out,
when the times of refreshing shall
come from the presence of the Lord.
And he shall send Jesus Christ, which
before was preached unto you.
ACTS 3:19-20

Thou, which hast shewed me great
and sore troubles, shalt quicken me
again, and shalt bring me up again
from the depths of the earth.
PSALM 71:20

For I have satiated the weary soul, and
I have replenished every sorrowful soul.
JEREMIAH 31:25

Reward

Blessed are the peacemakers: for they
shall be called the children of God.
MATTHEW 5:9

Say ye to the righteous, that it shall
be well with him: for they shall
eat the fruit of their doings.
ISAIAH 3:10

To him that soweth righteousness
shall be a sure reward.
PROVERBS 11:18

Verily there is a reward for the righteous.
PSALM 58:11

He that hath pity upon the poor
lendeth unto the LORD; and that which
he hath given will he pay him again.
PROVERBS 19:17

Yet surely my judgment is with
the LORD, and my work with my God.
ISAIAH 49:4

The LORD render to every man his righteousness and his faithfulness.
1 SAMUEL 26:23

He that handleth a matter wisely shall find good: and whoso trusteth in the LORD, happy is he.
PROVERBS 16:20

But love ye your enemies, and do good, and lend, hoping for nothing again; and your reward shall be great.
LUKE 6:35

That thine alms may be in secret: and thy Father which seeth in secret himself shall reward thee openly.
MATTHEW 6:4

Believe in the LORD your God, so shall ye be established; believe his prophets, so shall ye prosper.
2 CHRONICLES 20:20

To them who by patient continuance in well doing seek for glory and honour and immortality, eternal life.
ROMANS 2:7

And, behold, I come quickly; and my reward is with me, to give every man according as his work shall be.
REVELATION 22:12

Blessed is he that considereth the poor: the LORD will deliver him in time of trouble. The LORD will preserve him, and keep him alive; and he shall be blessed upon the earth.
PSALM 41:1-2

For God is not unrighteous to forget your work and labour of love, which ye have shewed toward his name, in that ye have ministered to the saints.
HEBREWS 6:10

And whosoever shall give to drink unto one of these little ones a cup of cold water only in the name of a disciple, verily I say unto you, he shall in no wise lose his reward.
MATTHEW 10:42

O the LORD search the heart, I try the reins, even to give every man according to his ways, and according to the fruit of his doings.
JEREMIAH 17:10

Salvation

Truly my soul waiteth upon God:
from him cometh my salvation. He only
is my rock and my salvation; he is my
defence; I shall not be greatly moved.
PSALM 62:1-2

For God is my King of old, working
salvation in the midst of the earth.
PSALM 74:12

Look unto me, and be ye saved,
all the ends of the earth: for I am
God, and there is none else.
ISAIAH 45:22

For God so loved the world, that
he gave his only begotten Son, that
whosoever believeth in him should not
perish, but have everlasting life.
JOHN 3:16

For unto us a child is born, unto us a
son is given: and the government shall
be upon his shoulder: and his name
shall be called Wonderful, Counsellor,
The mighty God, The everlasting
Father, The Prince of Peace.
ISAIAH 9:6

I that speak in righteousness,
mighty to save.
ISAIAH 63:1

Therefore if any man be in Christ, he is
a new creature: old things are passed
away; behold, all things are become
new. And all things are of God.
2 CORINTHIANS 5:17-18

Yet I will rejoice in the LORD,
I will joy in the God of my salvation.
HABAKKUK 3:18

But I have trusted in thy mercy; my heart shall rejoice in thy salvation.
PSALM 13:5

I will greatly rejoice in the LORD, my soul shall be joyful in my God; for he hath clothed me with the garments of salvation, he hath covered me with the robe of righteousness.
ISAIAH 61:10

In God is my salvation.
PSALM 62:7

It is good that a man should both hope and quietly wait for the salvation of the LORD.
LAMENTATIONS 3:26

For God hath not appointed us to wrath, but to obtain salvation by our Lord Jesus Christ.
1 THESSALONIANS 5:9

So Christ was once offered to bear
the sins of many; and unto them that
look for him shall he appear the second
time without sin unto salvation.
HEBREWS 9:28

For God sent not his Son into the world
to condemn the world; but that the
world through him might be saved.
JOHN 3:17-18

Call upon me in the day of trouble: I will
deliver thee, and thou shalt glorify me.
PSALM 50:15

Behold, God is my salvation; I will
trust, and not be afraid: for the LORD
JEHOVAH is my strength and my song;
he also is become my salvation.
ISAIAH 12:2

Strength

$\mathcal{I}$ can do all things through Christ
which strengtheneth me.
PHILIPPIANS 4:13

$\mathcal{F}$ear thou not; for I am with thee:
be not dismayed; for I am thy God: I
will strengthen thee; yea, I will help
thee; yea, I will uphold thee with the
right hand of my righteousness.
ISAIAH 41:10

$\mathcal{T}$he joy of the LORD is your strength.
NEHEMIAH 8:10

$\mathcal{B}$ut the Lord is faithful, who shall
stablish you, and keep you from evil.
2 THESSALONIANS 3:3

$\mathcal{I}$n quietness and in confidence
shall be your strength.
Isaiah 30:15

$\mathcal{G}$od is my strength and power:
and he maketh my way perfect.
2 Samuel 22:33

$\mathcal{H}$e hath made the earth by his
power, he hath established the world
by his wisdom, and hath stretched
out the heavens by his discretion.
Jeremiah 10:12

$\mathcal{S}$trengthened with all might, according
to his glorious power ... giving
thanks unto the Father, which hath
made us meet to be partakers of the
inheritance of the saints in light.
Colossians 1:11-12

Be strong in the Lord, and in
the power of his might.
EPHESIANS 6:10

The LORD shall guide thee continually,
and satisfy thy soul in drought, and
make fat thy bones: and thou shalt
be like a watered garden, and like a
spring of water, whose waters fail not.
ISAIAH 58:11

The LORD is my strength and song.
EXODUS 15:2

The LORD God is my strength, and he will
make my feet like hinds' feet, and he will
make me to walk upon mine high places.
HABAKKUK 3:19

They that wait upon the LORD shall
renew their strength; they shall
mount up with wings as eagles; they
shall run, and not be weary; and
they shall walk, and not faint.
ISAIAH 40:31

With whom my hand shall
be established: mine arm also
shall strengthen him.
PSALM 89:21

Blessed is the man that walketh
not in the counsel of the ungodly,
nor standeth in the way of sinners,
nor sitteth in the seat of the scornful.
But his delight is in the law of the LORD;
and in his law doth he meditate day
and night. And he shall be like a tree
planted by the rivers of water,
that bringeth forth his fruit in his
season; his leaf also shall not wither;
and whatsoever he doeth shall prosper.
PSALM 1:1-3

Wherefore take unto you the
whole armour of God, that ye may
be able to withstand in the evil day,
and having done all, to stand.
EPHESIANS 6:13

It is God that girdeth me with
strength, and maketh my way perfect.
PSALM 18:32

Support

For the LORD your God,
he it is that fighteth for you,
as he hath promised you.
JOSHUA 23:10

For the LORD shall be thy
confidence, and shall keep
thy foot from being taken.
PROVERBS 3:26

Bear ye one another's burdens,
and so fulfil the law of Christ.
GALATIANS 6:2

My God shall supply all your
need according to his riches
in glory by Christ Jesus.
PHILIPPIANS 4:19

Not that we are sufficient of ourselves
to think any thing as of ourselves;
but our sufficiency is of God.
2 CORINTHIANS 3:5

Thou shalt remember the LORD
thy God: for it is he that giveth
thee power to get wealth.
DEUTERONOMY 8:18

He giveth power to the faint;
and to them that have no might
he increaseth strength.
ISAIAH 40:29

The steps of a good man are ordered by
the LORD: and he delighteth in his way.
PSALM 37:23

The LORD is good, a strong hold in
the day of trouble; and he knoweth
them that trust in him.
NAHUM 1:7

To do good and to communicate
forget not: for with such sacrifices
God is well pleased.
HEBREWS 13:16

The God of all grace, who hath
called us unto his eternal glory by
Christ Jesus, after that ye have
suffered a while, make you perfect,
stablish, strengthen, settle you.
1 PETER 5:10

They that trust in the LORD shall
be as mount Zion, which cannot be
removed, but abideth for ever.
PSALM 125:1

Thou shalt also decree a thing, and
it shall be established unto thee: and
the light shall shine upon thy ways.
JOB 22:28

Teamwork

If there be therefore any consolation in Christ, if any comfort of love, if any fellowship of the Spirit, if any bowels and mercies, fulfil ye my joy, that ye be likeminded, having the same love, being of one accord, of one mind.
PHILIPPIANS 2:1-2

How good and how pleasant it is for brethren to dwell together in unity!
PSALM 133:1

Christ from whom the whole body fitly joined together and compacted by that which every joint supplieth, according to the effectual working in the measure of every part, maketh increase of the body unto the edifying of itself in love.
EPHESIANS 4:16

The manifestation of the Spirit is given to every man to profit withal.
1 CORINTHIANS 12:7

For where two or three are
gathered together in my name,
there am I in the midst of them.
MATTHEW 18:20

Endeavouring to keep the unity
of the Spirit in the bond of peace.
EPHESIANS 4:3

O magnify the LORD with me,
and let us exalt his name together.
PSALM 34:3

Now the God of patience
and consolation grant you to
be likeminded one toward
another according to Christ Jesus.
ROMANS 15:5

For as the body is one, and hath many members, and all the members of that one body, being many, are one body: so also is Christ.
1 CORINTHIANS 12:12

And let us consider one another to provoke unto love and to good works: not forsaking the assembling of ourselves together.
HEBREWS 10:24-25

Two are better than one; because they have a good reward for their labour. For if they fall, the one will lift up his fellow.
ECCLESIASTES 4:9-10

If the whole body were an eye, where were the hearing? If the whole were hearing, where were the smelling? But now hath God set the members every one of them in the body, as it hath pleased him.
1 CORINTHIANS 12:17-18

Trust

Trust in the LORD with all thine heart;
and lean not unto thine own
understanding. In all thy ways
acknowledge him, and he
shall direct thy paths.
PROVERBS 3:5-6

Blessed is that man that
maketh the LORD his trust.
PSALM 40:4

Blessed is the man that trusteth in
the LORD, and whose hope the LORD is.
JEREMIAH 17:7

The LORD is good, a strong hold in
the day of trouble; and he knoweth
them that trust in him.
NAHUM 1:7

Commit thy works unto the Lord,
and thy thoughts shall be established.
PROVERBS 16:3

Every good gift and every perfect gift
is from above, and cometh down from
the Father of lights, with whom is no
variableness, neither shadow of turning.
JAMES 1:17

Cause me to hear thy lovingkindness
in the morning; for in thee do I trust.
PSALM 143:8

For I am the LORD, I change not.
MALACHI 3:6

They that know thy name will put
their trust in thee: for thou, LORD,
hast not forsaken them that seek thee.
PSALM 9:10

Understanding

As one whom his mother
comforteth, so will I comfort you;
and ye shall be comforted.
ISAIAH 66:13

God is mighty in strength and wisdom.
JOB 36:5

Blessed are the merciful: for
they shall obtain mercy.
MATTHEW 5:7

The righteous considereth
the cause of the poor.
PROVERBS 29:7

He that giveth unto the
poor shall not lack.
PROVERBS 28:27

For in that he himself hath
suffered being tempted, he is able to
succour them that are tempted.
HEBREWS 2:18

The LORD GOD hath given me
the tongue of the learned, that I
should know how to speak a word
in season to him that is weary.
ISAIAH 50:4

Finally, be ye all of one mind, having
compassion one of another, love as
brethren, be pitiful, be courteous.
1 PETER 3:8

With everlasting kindness will I have mercy
on thee, saith the Lord thy Redeemer.
ISAIAH 54:8

For he hath not despised nor
abhorred the affliction of the afflicted;
neither hath he hid his face from him;
but when he cried unto him, he heard.
PSALM 22:24

The LORD openeth the eyes of the blind:
the LORD raiseth them that are bowed
down: the LORD loveth the righteous.
PSALM 146:8

The LORD is nigh unto them that
are of a broken heart; and saveth
such as be of a contrite spirit.
PSALM 34:18

Values

$\mathcal{B}$y pureness, by knowledge,
by long suffering, by kindness,
by the Holy Ghost, by love unfeigned.
2 Corinthians 6:6

$\mathcal{G}$iving all diligence, add to your faith
virtue; and to virtue knowledge.
2 Peter 1:5

$\mathcal{T}$herefore all things whatsoever
ye would that men should do to
you, do ye even so to them.
Matthew 7:12

$\mathcal{L}$et love be without dissimulation.
Abhor that which is evil; cleave
to that which is good.
Romans 12:9

A little that a righteous man hath is better than the riches of many wicked.
<small>PSALM 37:16</small>

*F*or the LORD God is a sun and shield: the LORD will give grace and glory: no good thing will he withhold from them that walk uprightly.
<small>PSALM 84:11</small>

*B*ut the path of the just is as the shining light, that shineth more and more unto the perfect day.
<small>PROVERBS 4:18</small>

*L*et him that stole steal no more: but rather let him labour, working with his hands the thing which is good, that he may have to give to him that needeth.
<small>EPHESIANS 4:28</small>

With all lowliness and meekness,
with longsuffering, forbearing
one another in love.
EPHESIANS 4:2

Blessed are the peacemakers: for they
shall be called the children of God.
MATTHEW 5:9

Whose adorning let it not be that
outward adorning of plaiting the hair,
and of wearing of gold, or of putting
on of apparel; but let it be the hidden
man of the heart, in that which is
not corruptible, even the ornament
of a meek and quiet spirit, which is
in the sight of God of great price.
1 PETER 3:3-4

Blessed are they that keep
judgment, and he that doeth
righteousness at all times.
PSALM 106:3

Wisdom

If any of you lack wisdom, let him ask of God, that giveth to all men liberally, and upbraideth not; and it shall be given him.
JAMES 1:5

So shall the knowledge of wisdom be unto thy soul: when thou hast found it, then there shall be a reward, and thy expectation shall not be cut off.
PROVERBS 24:14

They that be wise shall shine as the brightness of the firmament; and they that turn many to righteousness as the stars for ever and ever.
DANIEL 12:3

So teach us to number our days, that we may apply our hearts unto wisdom.
PSALM 90:12

With him is wisdom and strength,
he hath counsel and understanding.
JOB 12:13

The wisdom that is from above is first
pure, then peaceable, gentle, and easy to
be intreated, full of mercy and good fruits,
without partiality, and without hypocrisy.
JAMES 3:17

Happy is the man that
findeth wisdom, and the man
that getteth understanding.
PROVERBS 3:13

Thou through thy commandments
hast made me wiser than mine
enemies: for they are ever with me.
PSALM 119:98

For the LORD giveth wisdom: out
of his mouth cometh knowledge
and understanding.
PROVERBS 2:6

*F*orsake her not, and she shall preserve thee: love her, and she shall keep thee. Wisdom is the principal thing; therefore get wisdom: and with all thy getting get understanding.
PROVERBS 4:6-7

*W*hoso is wise, and will observe these things, even they shall understand the lovingkindness of the LORD.
PSALM 107:43

*T*hat their hearts might be comforted, being knit together in love, and unto all riches of the full assurance of understanding, to the acknowledgement of the mystery of God, and of the Father, and of Christ; in whom are hid all the treasures of wisdom and knowledge.
COLOSSIANS 2:2-3

*T*he foolishness of God is wiser than men; and the weakness of God is stronger than men.
1 CORINTHIANS 1:25

Work

Whatsoever ye do, do it heartily,
as to the Lord, and not unto men.
COLOSSIANS 3:23

Be strong, all ye people of the land,
saith the LORD, and work: for I am
with you, saith the LORD of hosts.
HAGGAI 2:4

The LORD thy God shall bless thee
in all thine increase, and in all the
works of thine hands, therefore
thou shalt surely rejoice.
DEUTERONOMY 16:15

The LORD shall open unto thee his
good treasure, the heaven to give
the rain unto thy land in his season,
and to bless all the work of thine
hand: and thou shalt lend unto many
nations, and thou shalt not borrow.
DEUTERONOMY 28:12

That ye study to be quiet, and to do your own business, and to work with your own hands, as we commanded you; that ye may walk honestly toward them that are without, and that ye may have lack of nothing.

1 THESSALONIANS 4:11-12

Be ye strong therefore, and let not your hands be weak: for your work shall be rewarded.

2 CHRONICLES 15:7

For he that is entered into his rest, he also hath ceased from his own works, as God did from his.

HEBREWS 4:10

It is vain for you to rise up early, to sit up late, to eat the bread of sorrows: for so he giveth his beloved sleep.

PSALM 127:2

Every man also to whom God hath given riches and wealth, and hath given him power to eat thereof, and to take his portion, and to rejoice in his labour; this is the gift of God.

ECCLESIASTES 5:19